Batsford Chess Library

Beating the Caro-Kann

Vassilios Kotronias

An Owl Book
Henry Holt and Company
New York

To Aspasia and Adoria

Henry Holt and Company, Inc.
Publishers since 1866
115 West 18th Street
New York, New York 10011

First published in the United States in 1994 by
Henry Holt and Company, Inc.
Originally published in Great Britain in 1994 by
B. T. Batsford Ltd.

Library of Congress Catalog Card Number: 93-80834

ISBN 0-8050-3284-3 (An Owl Book: pbk.)

First American Edition—1994

Printed in the United Kingdom
All first editions are printed on acid-free paper. ∞

10 9 8 7 6 5 4 3 2 1

Adviser: R. D. Keene, GM, OBE
Technical Editor: Graham Burgess

Contents

Bibliography

ChessBase

Periodicals
Inside Chess up to issue 9/1993
Informator 1-57

Books
Chernev, *Capablanca's Best Chess Endings*, Dover 1982
Karpov, *The Semi-Open Game in Action*, Batsford 1988
Keene & Taulbut, *How to Play the Caro-Kann Defence*, Batsford 1989
Seirawan, *Caro-Kann B12*, Sahovski Informator 1993
Speelman, *New Ideas in the Caro-Kann Defence*, Batsford 1992
Suetin, *Caro-Kann Defence*, Batsford 1988
Varnusz, *Play the Caro-Kann*, Pergamon Press, 1982

Acknowledgements

The author wishes to thank Ilias Kourkounakis for extensive editing of the text and help with the diagrams.

Symbols

+-	White is winning
±	White is clearly better
±	White is slightly better
=	The position is equal
∓	Black is slightly better
∓	Black is clearly better
-+	Black is winning
+	Check
#	Mate
!	Good move
?	Bad move
!!	Excellent move
??	Blunder
!?	Interesting move
?!	Dubious move
OL	Olympiad
Ch	Championship
IZ	Interzonal
Z	Zonal
corr.	Correspondence

Introduction

Books on openings usually end up in a dusty corner in one's library, especially nowadays. The reason is that chess theory develops like a monstrous creature, bombarded by computer information containing tens of thousands of games. Unlike good old times, main lines change with lightning speed and paths thought to be forgotten provide raw material for the experts. In fact there is nothing wrong with modern informatics, because chess is a scientific game and has to go on like that; the negative aspects of it are revealed when one spurns what is essential for the sake of 'ephemeral wisdom', and that characterizes many players of the new generation.

When I started writing this book, I understood the need to emphasize the ideas governing an opening variation. Therefore these ideas are presented separately (Chapter 1), since I think they form the most valuable part of the whole material; but the main reason is that the readers should be able to get a general picture of the various motifs that would help them evaluate a certain position. If they manage to do so, the purpose of this book will be fulfilled.

Chapters 2 to 6 feature the current status of theory in the variation suggested. An effort has been made to cover all gaps and present a complete repertoire for White. This doesn't mean I lost my objectivity; on the contrary, a reappraisal was made in positions previously dismissed as clearly bad for Black. From this point of view, this book can serve as a useful guide for those who wish to update their archives and spot the critical positions. Emphasis has been given in supportive analysis, a necessary tool for one's homework, and I hopefully expect it will prove so, combined with the introductory ideas.

As usual in the Batsford series of *"Beating the ... "* books, the material is presented in the form of complete games with all theoretical analysis incorporated in the notes. In this way the reader is presented with the most important links connecting the opening with typical middle-game positions and even the endgame. My selection was based mainly on the criterion that these games should exemplify White's strategy in the Caro Advance as well as possible. The book also contains some of White's remarkable failures, but I could not help including them as they are interesting from both a competitive and creative point of view. My main selection criterion for the games included in this book was the strength of the players, but care was taken not to leave out of this survey any games that might be interesting or theoretically important.

I hope that the material will prove to be stimulating and provide food for thought for those who wish to discover new ways of playing the variation with either color. For those who wish to be creative not only at the chessboard but also at home, I think the lines suggested are most suitable. After all, confidence in one's repertoire depends to a certain extent upon one's own personal analysis.

A Brief History

About the Caro–Kann in General

The Caro–Kann Defence was introduced into serious competition by the German players H. Caro and M. Kann in the last decades of the nineteenth century. As one might expect for an opening whose first principle was solidity, initially it was not greeted with great enthusiasm from the majority of chess fans. Nevertheless, its intrinsic merits soon caught the attention of some of the world's leading masters and it has been championed by many top players throughout the last hundred years. No less a player than Capablanca used it to good effect on several occasions, beating some of the most eminent grandmasters of his era with his customary virtuosity. A classic example, featured in this book, is his game against Nimzowitsch played in the New York super-tournament of 1927. A few years later Soviet GMs Botvinnik and Flohr took over, their scientific treatment of the game doing much to enhance the opening's popularity.

Since then, the Caro–Kann has been one of the main weapons in most World Champions' opening armoury. Botvinnik, Smyslov, Petrosian, Karpov and, occasionally, Kasparov have successfully defended the Black side, especially in matches at the highest level. I suspect this choice was not at all by chance, as the "Caro" is easier to play than the Sicilian, the Spanish or even the French, especially if Black is satisfied with a draw. However, the asymmetrical pawn structure which arises after 1 e4 c6 2 d4 d5 3 ♘c3 dxe4 means that Black can also play for a win, on the condition that he will accept a slightly worse position by avoiding liquidations during the early phases of the game.

Advance Variation

The Advance Variation (3 e5) is the most natural way to side-step Black's drawing tendencies and was seriously tested for the first time in the World Championship match between Tal and Botvinnik in 1961. Tal's

result with it was rather dis-
appointing (as was his whole
performance) and this was
probably responsible for the
line's abandonment in the next
twenty years. The line was
revived in the game Hort-
Seirawan, Bad Kissingen 1981,
which, however, resulted in a
brilliant win for Black. Whilst
one might have expected this
to have caused the revival to be
stillborn, in fact the opposite
was the case and it soon became apparent that Black could
not hold his own in the hair-
raising complications after 3 ...
♗f5 4 ♘c3 e6 5 g4!? ♗g6 6
♘ge2 c5 7 h4 cxd4?! 8 ♘xd4 h5
9 f4!. Later on, Black devised
ways of improving his play by
deviating on the 7th move and
by now the attention of White
players has switched to more
positional (and safer) paths.

Over the past decade, the
above mentioned system (starting with 4 ♘c3 e6 5 g4!?) was
mainly championed by the
Dutch GM and twice Candi-
dates' finalist Jan Timman. He
contributed a lot to its development with many interesting

novelties, but in most of the
games he failed to reap the
fruits of his labour since some
positions are easier to play with
Black, even if he stands objectively worse! This might seem a
bit discouraging to the average
player, but one should not
forget that the primary purpose
of chess analysis should be to
heal our weaknesses rather
than improve our strengths.

My personal experience with
the variation, especially the
alternative 4 ... ♕b6, taught me
that one should not trust
results but only objective
analysis. I started playing the
Advance in 1986; at the time
nobody would accept that 5
♗d3!? could lead to some sort
of game for White. Today, I
think that the move is worthy
of an !? and tomorrow – who
knows? – the evaluation might
change again. On the strength
of the analysis presented in this
book, it is my firm belief that 4
♘c3 is at least equal to the
alternatives and I hope that
readers will add their own
contribution to the history of
this topical opening.

1 Ideas in the Advance Variation

The Caro has long been considered one of Black's main defences against 1 e4. World Champions Capablanca, Botvinnik and Karpov have been its regular practitioners, which speaks itself for the soundness of the system and its particular merits: solidity, clarity and controlled aggresion. Contrary to the typical French Defence scenario, the light-squared bishop can develop freely along the c8-h3 diagonal and the struggle is of an open nature with clear-cut aims.

The Advance Variation is characterized by the move 3 e5, partly closing the centre. In that sense it is not a typical Caro-Kann and might cause discomfort to players whose main attraction to the opening was its simplicity. Also, Black is denied the traditional counterplay along the d- and (possibly) g-files as well as the square f6 for his knight's development.

In comparison with the French Advance, Black has acquired the privilege of developing his bishop on f5. How-

ever, this does not automatically mean that he has also managed to solve all his opening problems: he is a tempo down in the fight for the center with the break ... c5 and the bishop's position might turn out to be vulnerable. The purpose of this section is not to give concrete evaluations regarding these questions, but to examine typical situations with a view to helping readers in their assessments.

The Centre

The situation in the centre is always a major factor, defining the character of the chess struggle. In our case, the 'Nimzowitsch' pawn structure (d4, e5 for White, e6, d5 for Black) means that White will have to meet the thrusts ... c6-c5 or ... f7-f6 to his center and shape accordingly his own plans. These involve f2-f4-f5, hitting the base of Black's pawn chain, as well as expansion on the kingside with gains of time on the enemy bishop.

Sometimes White exchanges the light-squared bishops in

return for a space and time advantage. Then his proper reaction to Black's central thrusts differs; it has to do more with piece manoeuvring rather than pawn storms.

Before going on, it should be noted that the main object of this book is to analyse positions where White develops his queen's knight on c3. Although White is deprived of the possibility c2-c3, fortifying his centre, he receives a lot of compensation in the form of quick development and excellent attacking chances.

Short's way of treating the position (♘f3 and ♗e2), although by far the most solid one, does not put Black under pressure right from the start. Therefore, it is a useful weapon only for those who wish to avoid complications at an early stage. It is outside the spirit of this book to suggest such a line, since it does not comply with the general directions of battling the Caro-Kann as they have already been described above.

In this part of the book, I wish to take a close look at various general situations White may encounter in practice. Here I have taken some liberties with the diagrams in order to add more emphasis to pawn structures and their transformations.

In our first diagram, Black

has chosen to attack the base of White's chain by ... c6-c5. It seems that this thrust is more effective here than in the French, as the bishop stands actively on g6 while White's centre lacks the protective c2-c3. However, appearances can be deceptive. White does not necessarily have to reinforce d4 with a pawn; a knight would be very strong there. In addition, Black has spent two tempi to get his pawn to c5 and its partner on e6 lacks the valuable protection a 'bad' bishop could provide. Not surprisingly, this invites White to attack with f2-f4-f5.

Diagram 2 shows the results

of a correct White strategy: the f-pawn has achieved the shutting in (even temporarily) of the black bishop, while putting e6 under serious pressure. The pressure can be increased by moves like ♘e2-f4 or ♗f1-h3, as captures on f5 weaken decisively the d5 pawn. Black's only chance is to strive for counterplay on the queenside by means of ... c5-c4, ... b7-b5 etc. (see also the section 'Flank Activity').

It goes without saying that an early ... c5xd4 favours White since his pieces become active and the thematic pawn advance f2-f4-f5 gains in strength.

Now we shall proceed to examine positions where Black challenges White's central superiority with ... f7-f6. Such a position can be seen in diagram 3.

3

Black's choice has a two-fold purpose: to create a mobile pawn-mass in the centre and simultaneously provide a safe spot for his bishop on f7. From that square the bishop also guards the newly-created

weakness on e6, albeit at some cost in mobility.

A typical structure often arising in practice is the one presented in diagram 4.

4

Black has achieved his aim of obtaining a pawn preponderance in the centre as White took back on e5 with the d-pawn. This is, however, better than f4xe5 which deprives White's position of its dynamism and leaves the e-pawn practically isolated, ... c6-c5 not being far away. White should now hurry to redeploy his knight to f3 via d4, preventing the positional threat ... g7-g5. If he fails to stop it, Black's bishop will be out for good after the forced recapture h5xg6 e.p.

Sometimes Black delays taking on e5, thinking that he has all the time in the world at his disposal. This is a risky strategy and White can take advantage of it by a timely capture on f6.

In the resulting positions (similar to diagram 5) White

has the better pawn formation and a potential passed pawn on the kingside. Black's e-pawn is backward, but advancing it creates a hole on f5 for White's knight. These factors in conjunction with a slight space advantage guarantee White the better game.

A doubtful experiment is when Black combines both pawn breaks, hoping to liquidate White's centre and finally occupy it. In that case, White should opt for a general liquidation that would make his development tell. A position like diagram 6 comes to mind.

As usual, the energetic advance of the f-pawn has

played an important rôle in the realization of White's plans. The central wall is falling apart, it only remains to be seen whether Black's exposure is of fatal dimensions.

So far we have only looked at positions with light-squared bishops on the board. Exchanging these bishops seems antipositional for White, but it can be justified if Black weakens his kingside or neglects his development. After all, White's remaining bishop is not that 'bad' if one compares its present mobility to its black counterpart. What White players should be aware of, is the potential danger of drifting into a passive ending, especially if the position in the centre stabilizes.

Diagram 7 features such an ending, with White having the inferior bishop and a permanent weakness on d4. This kind of endgame might be tenable, but it is obviously not in one's interests to suffer for a draw as White.

The new situation without light-squared bishops demands a slightly different approach but basically the principle is the same: open up the position when you have the chance! This means that White should avoid answering ... c6–c5 with c2–c3, as that would lead to a fixed central structure, identical to the one in the previous diagram. The pawn on d4 would be a constant worry, while the attack usually fails without the king's bishop.

Counterattacking by f2–f4–f5 is difficult to achieve since Black can intensify his control on f5 by ... g7–g6 and ... h7–h5 in combination with ... ♘g8–e7. This is the main difference from previous examples, when Black could not organize a similar defence, as the bishop on g6 was standing in the way.

A typical reaction to ... c6–c5 after the exchange of the light-squared bishops can be seen in the following diagram:

The knight has retreated to d1 in order to free the way for the c-pawn. White's queen stands excellently, pressing towards the kingside and at the same time indirectly helping central operations, since ... d5xc4 could be met with d4–d5. Also important is the preventive rôle of the pawn on a5, which stops the consolidating ... ♘d7–b6. In general, White's position holds good prospects for the coming complications.

If White is not prepared to answer ... c6–c5 with c2–c4 he should opt for the modest approach of capturing on c5 and playing with his pieces on the kingside (diagram 9).

After d4xc5, ♘f4–d3 strengthens both e5 and f2. The knight from c3 can be redeployed via e2 to the kingside, with good attacking chances. A final remark is that the ... f7–f6 break has been rendered more weakening than usual after the exchange of bishops. So Black avoids it unless White gets completely reckless.

Here, our examination of various central motifs comes to

an end. Evidently, it is difficult to cover all cases, but I think that the examples given are quite representative of what White should aim for, and what he should try to avoid.

Flank Activity

Space is, undoubtedly, the most double-edged element in the game of chess. Unlike tempi or material, rules cannot be made about its relative value and everything depends upon the placing of the pieces. Therefore, the players' ability to evaluate each specific situation is of paramount importance.

Regarding the Advance Caro, there is an important axiom related to the value of space: the side with more space in the centre can operate on either flank with greater ease. This axiom is confirmed repeatedly in this variation, as most flank attacks are launched by White.

White's kingside expansion is a standard method of flank activity and characterizes many lines of the variation as a whole. It is grounded on the fact that Black's bishop on f5 provides White with enough tempi for its realization, and has the two-fold purpose of restricting the bishop's mobility as well as inducing weaknesses in the opponent's pawn formation.

Diagram 10 features the starting position of White's

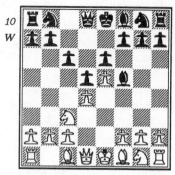

attack. After the bold g2-g4, forcing the retreat ... ♗f5-g6, comes the aggressive follow-up with ♘g1-e2 and h2-h4 *(11)*.

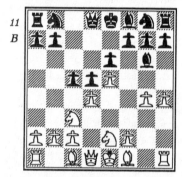

In this position, which we may consider as a *tabiya* for this opening, White is poised to answer the positional shot ... h7-h5, with ♘e2-f4, either winning a pawn or ruining the enemy pawn formation. Besides this risky attempt, Black can choose between:

a) ... f7-f6, hitting the centre at the cost of weakening e6;

b) ... c5xd4, enforcing ... h7-h5 by diverting the knight's attention from f4; and

c) ... h7-h6, giving up some space, but avoiding positional

concessions.

We have already witnessed during our discussion of central motifs, that as a rule White reacts properly to his opponent's plans by advancing his f-pawn. Cases (a) and (c) were partly covered there, while a brief comment was made on the negative aspects of possibility (b).

Evidently, it is impossible to examine wing operations separately from central affairs, especially when they have a decisive impact on each other. Thus, in the following we shall concentrate on positions with crystallized central structures, such as can be derived from options (b) and (c).

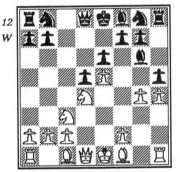

Diagram 12 features the starting position of a forced sequence, with White resorting to tactical measures in order to prove the viability of his system.

Black has just played ... h7-h5, hoping to turn White's kingside demonstration into a meaningless one. Were White

now to play g4-g5, his attack would be stopped dead in its tracks leaving a gruesome weakness on f5 as its only recollection. However, the newly established knight on d4 allows White a strong, albeit familiar, advance.

1 f4! hxg4 2 ♗b5+ ♘d7 3 f5! ♖xh4 4 ♖f1! exf5 5 e6

The complications are definitely in White's favour, as is demonstrated in Game 5, Nagel-Wouters and the extensive analysis included therein.

In the above example, White had to rely solely on tactics to avoid falling into an inferior position. The disadvantage of Black's idea was that he conceded the square d4 to the white knight with loss of tempo, thus relaxing the central pressure and creating a strong base for White's operations. Black may deny White using this square by a timely ... c5-c4, especially when both sides castle long. Then, relaxing the central pressure is more justified as the resulting pawn phalanx points menacingly at the white king.

In diagram 13 Black is ready for a massive assault on the queenside by ... ♕b6-a6 and ... b7-b5-b4. White's pawn already stands on f5, so ♘e2-f4, intensifying the pressure on e6, seems appropriate: it normally results in the pawn reaching f7 after Black sacrifices (cor-

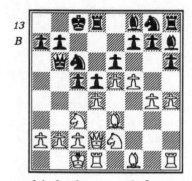

rectly) both e– and f–pawns. Since releasing the h7 bishop adds yet another weapon to Black's armoury, White must be aware that investing a piece would rather be necessary if he wants to stave off the mating threats. As is customary for such races, play becomes highly unbalanced; nevertheless the pawn on f7 might prove an important long–term asset (for a detailed analysis see the second match game Timman–Seirawan, Game 10).

If the light–squared bishops have been exchanged, White obviously lacks a target for an analogous expansion on the kingside. However, the bishops' absence allows White to carry out a different plan with a view to gaining space on the other wing. Take for instance the case of diagram 14:

Here the conditions are ideal for White to achieve his aims. Black has spent too much time creating a strongpoint on f5, thus neglecting the mobilization of his queenside. White can take advantage of this by playing ...

1 b3! ♘d7 **2 c4** ♘f8 **3** ♗d2 ♘g6 **4 c5±**

as Black is unable during this sequence to react successfully by ... c6–c5.

Finally, an exceptional case, with White attacking on the queenside and all pieces still on board can be found in the following example:

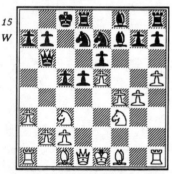

Black needs just one tempo to consolidate his central position by playing ... ♘e7–c6. White must prevent this, so the energetic **1 b4!** is called for, sacrificing a pawn to open lines against the enemy king. This move has also the additional advantage of breaking up Black's central pawn front, consequently freeing d4 for use by White's pieces. All in all, a promising attack is in sight, requiring only a tiny material investment on White's part.

So far, so good: attacking ideas have formulated the main part of our discussion. But as Nimzowitsch pointed out many years ago, chess is not only attack and defence; it is prevention and prophylaxis as well. Sometimes, White has to be modest and think about stopping Black's counterplay before going on with his own plans.

A case where flank activity has strictly a preventive rôle can be seen in the following diagram.

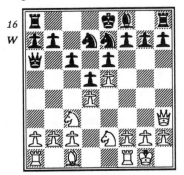

16
W

While it is clear that White's future lies on the kingside, he goes in for the paradoxical 1 a4. In fact this is not an attacking gesture, but a solid way to take the sting out of ... c6-c5 which would now be met strongly by ♘c3-b5. Also, White prepares

to exchange, if necessary, his inferior bishop by b2-b3, ♗c1-a3.

Certainly, Black can also try to be active on the queenside. We have already witnessed the case of diagram 13, with Black launching a dangerous attack on the white king; however, in principle queenside activity backfires if there are no concrete targets and freedom of movement in his interior lines:

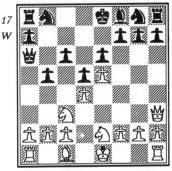

17
W

Diagram 17 features a space-gaining effort on the queenside. Black has just played ... b7-b5, thinking he will get away with it, in view of the closed nature of the position. But in fact, such reasoning is incorrect, since sooner or later ... c6-c5 has to occur and Black's demonstration will prove weakening and time-consuming.

The reader might have noticed that there was hardly any mention of White attacks on the kingside without pawns. As a matter of fact, this is a rare bird in the Advance Variation and is going to be exam-

ined in the "Manoeuvres" section.

Strongpoints –
Piece Exchanges

Securing strongpoints for one's
minor pieces is a common
theme in most semi-open Take
for example the Scheveningen
Variation of the Sicilian, where
it is a customary idea for Black
to create an outpost for his
knight on e5, in front of an
isolated white e-pawn (by ...
e6–e5xf4); to achieve this, he
usually conceeds a correspond-
ingly strong square for White
on d5. In our case, typical
squares for outposts derive
from the nature of the central
pawn formation, and are d4 for
White and f5 for Black.

It is well known that in
French-like pawn structures
the square d4 can become a
useful base of operations for
White's pieces. According to
Nimzowitsch, · White should
always keep a firm control on
d4 and e5 so that when Black
tries to liquidate his central
pawns these squares can be
taken up by pieces. In the
French hybrid of the Caro
Advance, occurring after 3 ...
c5?! 4 dxc5!, White has enough
time to carry out these ideas,
as Black has lost a tempo
without causing any disruption
in his opponent's development.

Diagram 18 features the final
position of a piece of analysis

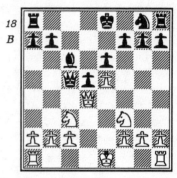

18
B

by Pachman. White has complete domination of d4 since
Black has had to exchange the
dark-squared bishops in order
to recover his pawn. Pachman's
last move (♕d1–d4) indicates
his preference for a better
endgame, but also acceptable is
the Nimzowitschian approach,
with 0–0, ♖f1–e1, to be followed
by ♘c3–e2–d4. In both cases,
the superiority of knight vs
bishop is quite evident.

The knight on d4, apart from
its blockading duties, can serve
attacking purposes as well. We
have already witnessed the case
of diagram 12, where its func-
tion was to support the advance of White's f-pawn and
simultaneously attack e6, finally resulting in a sacrificial
breakthrough. Dramatic developments are not to be expected in the next example, but
the knight's rôle is very similar.

The main characteristic of
this position is the inclusion of
the move ... h7–h6 in Black's
defensive set-up. This inspires
White to attack either by push-

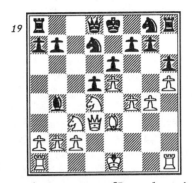

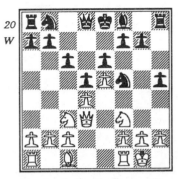

ing his pawn to f5, or by g4-g5-g6, exploiting the weakened light-square complex on Black's kingside. His knight is supremely placed for both plans, exerting pressure against the potential weakness on e6. It should be noted here that, despite the absence of the light-squared bishops, White's pawn advances are justifiable as Black cannot build the well-known defensive formation with pawns on g6 and h5.

As has already been mentioned, Black's traditional outpost in the center is the square f5. Occupation of this square by a knight presupposes an early exchange of the light-squared bishops. Black usually strengthens the knight's position by ... h7-h5, a typical case shown in diagram 20:

Black has accomplished his plan, albeit at the cost of a considerable amount of time. The knight stands beautifully on f5, but if White manages to exchange it, the disadvantages involved in ... h7-h5 will become

apparent. A thematic continuation would be 1 ♘e2 ♘d7 2 ♘g3 g6 3 ♘xf5 gxf5 4 ♗g5 ♗e7 5 h4! inflicting some permanent changes on the character of the game:

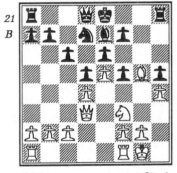

Black's outpost on f5 has disappeared, in return for the opening of the g-file. However, White's control of g5 nullifies Black's attacking chances, so what counts in the long run is the weakness on h5 as well as the insecurity of the black king. To take advantage of these factors, White should try to open up the game on the queenside as quickly as possible.

The Caro Advance is a dynamic opening, but hardly an antipositional one. Not rarely, White sacrifices a pawn at an early stage for concrete positional gains.

The following example is quite characteristic: after the moves 1 e4 c6 2 d4 d5 3 e5 ♗f5 4 ♘c3 ♕b6 5 ♗d3 ♗xd3 6 ♕xd3 e6 7 ♘ge2 ♘e7 8 0-0 ♘d7 9 a4 a6 10 ♕h3 ♘f5 11 a5 ♕d8 12 ♘d1 c5 13 c4 dxc4 14 d5 ♕h4 15 dxe6 fxe6 16 ♕c3 ♘d4 17 ♘xd4 ♕xd4 18 ♕h3 ♕xe5 19 ♘e3 ♗e7 20 ♘xc4 ♕d5 21 b3 we have reached the position in diagram 22 (extensive analysis of this specific sequence is provided in Game 15, Kotronias-Tukmakov.

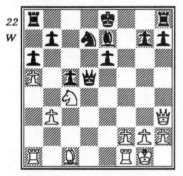

22
W

White is a pawn down, but his knight is ideally placed on c4, eyeing the weak dark squares on Black's queenside. Black's b- and c-pawns are practically isolated and his e-pawn irremediably weak. Although it cannot be claimed with any certainty that White enjoys an advantage here, it is obvious that the burden of proof lies on Black's side.

A difficult problem one has to solve during over the board play is the question of exchanges. The main reason for this is that the relative value of each minor piece is sensitive, in view of the complicated and constantly transforming pawn structures. Mastering this subject requires the development of one's intuition, together with knowledge of some typical cases.

A) Exchange of Light-Squared Bishops

Referring to this exchange has surely become a routine, but the careful reader must have noticed the reason for such an attitude: exchanging one's own good bishop is against the principles of classical theory, so it is of major importance to explain how this is balanced by other factors. A most enlightening case occurs as early as the fourth move (see diagram 23).

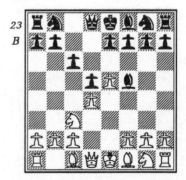

23
B

The normal continuation for Black would be 4 ... e6, demanding a deep knowledge of the complications arising after 5 g4 ♗g6 6 ♘ge2 c5 7 h4. However, if the second player is reluctant to enter this line he may try a semi-waiting move such as 4 ... ♕b6 or 4 ... h5. Then 5 ♗d3 becomes feasible, but only because Black was first to violate a so-called classical rule: 4 ... ♕b6 commits the queen too early, while 4 ... h5 weakens Black's kingside without furthering his development. Under the circumstances it is not surprising that the 'anti-positional' 5 ♗d3 should work, as after 5 ... ♗xd3 6 ♕xd3 Black's only developed piece is removed and White's queen is given access to the weakened sector. In fact, 4 ... ♕b6 creates no weaknesses in the structural sense, but the queen's absence from the kingside will probably make itself felt later on.

Exchanging the light-squared bishops is also justified if White has induced a favourable fixing of Black's kingside pawns. A relevant case appears in the following situation (diagram 24).

White plays 1 ♗d3 in order to get rid of the annoying bishop on h7. After 1 ... ♗xd3 2 ♕xd3 the position is similar to diagram 19, Black's weaknesses being vulnerable not only in the resulting middle-

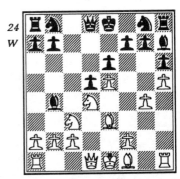

24
W

game, but in an ending as well.

B) Exchange of a Strongly Placed Knight

This is another recurring theme, as Black quite often establishes his knight on f5 in order to halt White's kingside aggression. White normally tries to exchange it, diagrams 20 and 21 featuring the starting position as well as results of such an effort. For more details see the next section.

C) Other Exchanges

Sometimes, Black gives up his dark-squared bishop for a white knight on c3. Like its distant relative from the Winawer, this exchange aims at a weakening of White's pawn structure, hoping to exploit it at a later stage. Under specific circumstances Black may succeed, but in general the fortification of White's centre, in conjuction with the usual time advantage he enjoys in the Advance Caro, allows him to exploit the bishop vs knight advantage.

Finally, ideas for White to trade his inferior bishop are not always out of the question, diagram 25 offering a typical example.

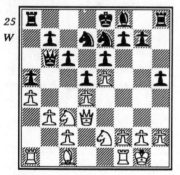

White can play 1 ♗a3 (1 ♗g5 is better, but only for tactical reasons – see the analysis of Kotronias-Orr, included in Game 15) carrying out the strategic plan already outlined during the discussion of diagram 16. Exchanging this bishop means that he will not have to worry any more about drifting in a worse ending, albeit at the disadvantage of easing Black's cramp a little.

Manoeuvres

The Caro Advance is an opening variation noted for its dynamism and versatility. There is no manoeuvring in the traditional sense, as the whole board is in an almost permanent state of flux and in almost every game we witness a body-to-body fight between the two armies. Thus, there are

no concrete positional targets in most of the sharp lines arising in the Advance Variation and this explains the lack of standard manoeuvres, contrary to openings such as the Tarrasch Defence in the Queen's Gambit, the Sämisch Variation of the Nimzo-Indian, etc.

The only lines where play takes a more or less positional character are those arising after an early exchange of the light-squared bishops. These positions require a different kind of approach, since the customary pawn storms would now fail to impress Black; his position is sufficiently solid to meet this kind of activity by setting up a successful blockade on the light squares. If White underestimates this fact he will soon run out of play on the kingside, as in the classic game Nimzowitsch-Capablanca, New York 1927:

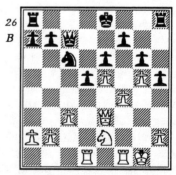

White's careless demonstration has ended up in a complete strategic disaster. Black has not only conquered the square f5 for his knight but, more importantly, has turned the tables as far as king safety is concerned. After **1 ... 0-0 2 ♘d4 ♛b6 3 ♖f2 ♖fc8**, Capablanca went on to win by penetrating through the c-file (the whole game is extensively analysed later on as Game 12, with some significant suggestions about misconceptions that have endured for decades regarding its opening stages).

Similar accidents are to be avoided if White understands the needs of the position for piece manoeuvring. Most of these manoeuvres aim at challenging Black's control of the f5 square, while others are associated with the idea of exerting pressure on Black's kingside.

In diagram 20 we made our first acquaintance with the above-mentioned type of manoeuvre. White resorted to ♘c3-e2-g3 which, as it turns out, has a two-fold purpose: to unblock the c-pawn for central action and to underline the weaknesses created by the move ... h7-h5. This manoeuvre signals the start of Black's difficulties, as after the normal continuation **1 ♘e2 ♘d7 2 ♘g3** he has to make a positional concession:

In the diagrammed position, Black is faced with the unpleasant dilemma of either opening up the f-file for White

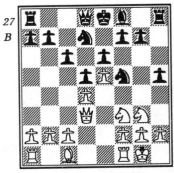

27
B

by 1 ... ♘xg3 2 fxg3, or allowing the weakening of his pawn structure after 1 ... g6 2 ♘xf5 gxf5. The first choice is clearly inferior as 1 ... ♘xg3 2 fxg3 ♗e7 runs into 3 h4! with a dangerous attacking position for White. In that case the shortcomings of ... h7-h5 become particularly felt, since the g5 point turns into a fearsome base of operations in White's hands.

The lesser evil is **1 ... g6**. After **2 ♘xf5 gxf5 3 ♗g5 ♗e7 4 h4** we reach a position that has been briefly discussed under diagram 21.

White's manoeuvre has paid off well, as he has obtained a firm grip on the kingside. Black's only counterplay is based on the fact that the guard of the g-file has been removed and an avenue towards the white king has been opened, but the plan ... ♘d7-f8-h7 would be too slow to enjoy realistic chances of success. In the meantime White may generate play on the queenside, a sample line being **4 ... ♘f8 5 b4 ♘h7** (5 ... ♘g6 6 g3 f4 7 b5±; 5 ... b5? 6 a4±) **6 ♗xe7 ♕xe7 7 b5 cxb5** (7 ... c5 8 c4±; 7 ... ♖c8 8 c4±) **8 ♕xb5+ ♕d7 9 ♖fb1** with an endgame advantage due to the weakness on h5.

In some lines we have a slightly different configuration of White's pieces, the king's knight standing on e2 instead of f3. Although ♘g1-e2 seems artificial, it has the advantageous point of allowing a queen transfer to the kingside, presumably on h3. From that square the queen may help in evicting the black knight from f5:

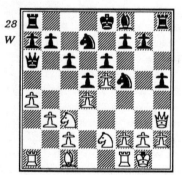

28
W

With **1 g4** White exploits the pin on the h-file, forcing Black to admit that occupying f5 was premature. After **1 ... ♘e7 2 ♘g3 g6 3 ♗g5** the position is clearly in White's favour.

A disadvantage entailed in ♘g1-e2 is that it hinders the common manoeuvre ♘c3-e2-g3 aiming to exchange the knight

on f5 under favourable conditions. Although there is another route to do this by ♘c3-d1-e3, it is not always as efficient, the following example being the proof:

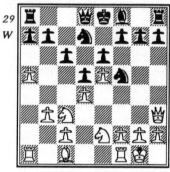

29
W

On **1 ♘d1** Black responds with **1 ... c5**, nipping in the bud the desired manoeuvre. White is forced to go in for wild complications with **2 c4 cxd4 3 cxd5 ♘xe5 4 dxe6 fxe6 5 ♘f4 ♕f6 6 ♖e1**, although his knight on d1 is a passive spectator for the time being. However, note that if White's b-pawn were still on its original square (as in diagram 8) he would enjoy a winning advantage in view of the extra possibility ♕h3-b3.

The type of game featured in the last few diagrams bears a close resemblance to positions from the French. In this respect, a knight on e2 might prove conveniently placed, as it suits White's plan to apply kingside pressure with the aid of his cavalry. The queen on h3 proves a useful coordinator of the play, supporting the knights' manoeuvres in tactical fashion:

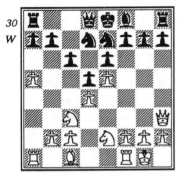

White starts with 1 ♘f4, toying with the ideas ♘f4-h5 and ♘f4xe6. Black would like to neutralize White's initiative by playing 1 ... ♘g6, but this is out of the question in view of the simple 2 ♘xg6, winning material. Also bad is 1 ... c5 2 ♘b5 ♘c6 3 ♘xe6 which merely helps to underline the powerful rôle of the queen on h3. Therefore, 1 ... ♘f5 is called for, although it does not really shake off White's grip on the position; after 2 ♘ce2 White completes his manoeuvre in an efficient way, preparing to meet 2 ... c5 with 3 c4, opening up the game for his own benefit.

The lack of typical manoeuvres in the hair-raising complications resulting after 3 ... ♗f5 4 ♘c3 e6 5 g4 has already been mentioned. An instructive piece of manoeuvring is the consolidating knight tour from diagram 4, but this is an isolated case depending upon the peculiarities of a specific situation. A rare instance of a motif applying in different lines involves manoeuvring with the king's rook along the third rank.

Consider the following case:

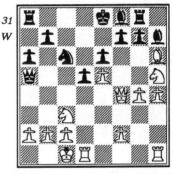

This position has been reached after 1 e4 c6 2 d4 d5 3 e5 ♗f5 4 ♘c3 e6 5 g4 ♗g6 6 ♘ge2 c5 7 h4 h5 8 ♘f4 ♗h7 9 ♘xh5 cxd4 10 ♕xd4 ♘c6 11 ♗b5 ♘ge7 12 ♗h6 a6 13 ♗xc6+ ♘xc6 14 ♕f4 ♖g8 15 0-0-0 ♕a5 (for a comprehensive coverage of the introductory moves consult Game 6, van der Wiel-Icklicki). Black has a strong attack in view of the open c-file and the activity of his pieces, but White is not without resources: with **16 ♖h3!** the king's rook is brought efficiently into the game, not only supporting his vulnerable queenside but also preparing to add pressure on f7 by ♖h3-f3.

Similar rook manoeuvres can be encountered in ... f7-f6 lines, as well as in the main 6 ... c5 line, resulting after 6 ... c5 7 h4 h6 8 ♗e3 ♛b6 etc. The main purpose of such a manoeuvre in these cases is defensive, a characteristic example being the following one. *(32)*:

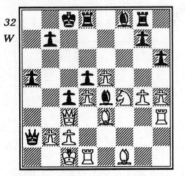

This position could have arisen in the game Prasad-Ravi, India 1991. Play had begun **1 e4 c6 2 d4 d5 3 e5 ♗f5 4 ♘c3 e6 5 g4 ♗g6 6 ♘ge2 c5 7 h4 h6 8 ♗e3 ♛b6 9 f4 ♘c6 10 f5** ♗h7 **11 ♛d2 0-0-0 12 0-0-0 c4 13 ♘f4 ♛a6 14 fxe6 ♘b4 15 exf7**, and now 15 ... ♘xa2+? **16 ♘xa2 ♛xa2 17 ♛c3 ♗e4 18 fxg8♛ ♖xg8 19 ♖h3 a5** would have reached the diagram.

Black has sacrificed a piece for what seems to be a virulent attack, but the rook on h3 proves its defensive value. After **20 ♗g1 ♗b4 21 ♛a3! ♗xa3 22 ♖xa3** White repulses all threats, entering an easily won ending.

At this point Chapter 1 of this book comes to an end, but it should be well digested before proceeding further: the ideas presented here are essential for a proper understanding of the opening lines suggested in the rest of the book.

2 The 4 ... e6 5 g4 ♗g6 6 ♘ge2 Variation

In the past few years the Advance Variation against the Caro has been seen more and more often at top level chess. GMs Timman, Short, Anand and Nunn have been its main adherents. Their results have been mixed, but on the whole, I think, White has satisfactory play.

The system characterized by the move 4 ♘c3 has recently fallen out of favour. However, a decline in popularity is not always the result of any fault of the opening: in this particular case the new plan with ♘g1-f3, ♗f1-e2 has scored well in practice, and consequently the attention of most Advance devotees has been drawn away from the 'old' line. I believe that such a tendency is not justified in terms of objective thinking. The variations starting with 4 ♘c3 are extremely rich in possibilities and definitely constitute the sharpest method available in White's arsenal. Black has to be superbly prepared in order to weather the storm at the early stages, but even that could prove insuffi-

cient against someone who has delved deeper into the intricacies of the position.

Alternatives to 6 ... c5 (Games 1-4)

Game 1
Vasiukov - Razuvaev
USSR 1981

1	e4	c6
2	d4	d5
3	e5	♗f5
4	♘c3	e6
5	g4	

With 5 g4 White declares his intentions for a complicated fight: he plans a development of his knight to e2, followed by a massive advance of his kingside pawns. The point of such a strategy lies in the insecure position of Black's bishop which White should exploit by either forcing Black to accept a weakness in his pawn structure or by gaining enough time to build a space advantage.

5	...	♗g6
6	♘ge2 (33)	
6	...	♗b4?!

The most usual continua-

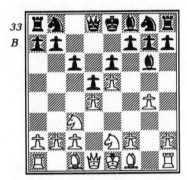

tions 6 ... f6 and 6 ... c5 are illustrated extensively in subsequent games. Other moves have failed to bring Black joy:

a) **6 ... ♕h4?! 7 ♗e3!** (sacrificing the pawn as on 7 ... ♕xg4?!, 8 ♕d2 to be followed by 9 0-0-0 gives excellent compensation; worse is 7 ♘f4 ♘h6 8 h3 ♗b4 9 ♗d2 ♘d7 10 ♘ce2 ♗xd2+ 11 ♕xd2 ♕e7 as played in van der Wiel–Timman, Brussels SWIFT blitz 1987) **7 ... ♘h6 8 ♗xh6! gxh6 9 ♘g3 ♗e7 10 f4 f6 11 ♗g2** and Black's position is riddled with weaknesses, Blumenfeld–Kasparian, USSR 1931.

b) **6 ... ♗e7!?** is analysed extensively in Game 2, Minasian–Miles.

c) Finally, **6 ... h6 7 h4 c5** transposes to 6 ... c5.

7 h4

Interesting, but probably inferior to the text is **7 a3!?**, despite White's success in the game dos Santos–Wallace, Guarapuava 1991, which continued 7 ... ♗xc3+ 8 ♘xc3 h5 9 h4 hxg4 10 ♕xg4 ♘e7 11 h5 ♖h7 12 ♗d3 ♗xd3 13 cxd3 ♘f5 14 ♗e3 ♘d7 15 0-0-0 ♕c7 16 ♔b1 0-0-0 *(34)*

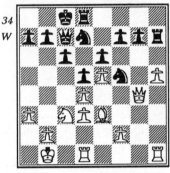

17 ♘xd5 ♘xe5 18 ♕xf5 exf5 19 ♘xc7 ♘g4 20 ♘b5 cxb5 21 ♖c1+ ♔d7 22 ♖c5 ♔e6 23 ♗g5 f6 24 ♖e1+ ♔f7 25 ♖c7+ ♔g8 26 ♗f4 ♘xf2 27 ♖ee7 ♘xd3 28 ♗d2 ♖xh5 29 ♖xg7+ ♔h8 30 ♗c3 ♘f4 31 ♖xb7 a6 32 ♖gf7 ♘d5 33 ♗a5 ♖e8 34 ♖bd7 f4 35 ♗d8 f3 36 ♗xf6+ ♘xf6 37 ♖xf6 ♖h1+ 38 ♔a2 ♖h3 39 d5 ♔g8 40 ♖g6+ ♔h8 41 ♖f6 ♔g8 42 ♖df7 ♖d8 43 ♖xf3 ♖xf3 44 ♖xf3 ♖xd5 45 ♖f6 a5 46 ♔b3 ♖d3+ 47 ♔c2 ♖d5 48 ♖a6 ♔f7?? (Black could have drawn with 48 ... a4) and White won on move 63. Despite the final result, it is clear that 7 h4 is a much safer move than 7 a3. With the latter, White adopted a risky strategy involving many pawn weaknesses and Black's play could certainly be improved upon.

Another move that has been essayed by White in this position is **7 ♘f4**, but it does not seem to be particularly dangerous. The game Djurhuus–

Fossan, Stavanger 1989, continued 7 ... ♘e7 8 h4 h6 9 h5 ♗e4
10 f3 ♗h7 11 ♗d3 ♘d7 12 ♗d2
♕c7 13 ♗xh7 ♖xh7 14 ♘ce
2 ♗xd2+ 15 ♕xd2 c5 16 c3 0-0-0
17 ♘d3 ♘c6 with an equal
game.

7	...	♗e4
8	♖h3	h5?!

A dubious experiment. Ac-
cording to Vasiukov, Black
should have been content with
the modest 8 ... h6. In the next
few moves White takes advantage of Black's adventurous
play in simple and powerful
fashion.

9   ♘g3! *(35)*

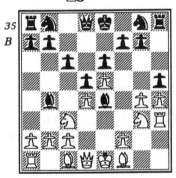

9   ...   c5

In the game Lee–Pieterse,
Dieren 1989, Black varied with
9 ... hxg4 10 ♕xg4 ♘e7, getting a good position after **11
♘h5?** ♔d7! and the game
ending as a draw after 12 ♗d3
♗xd3 13 ♖xd3 ♘f5 14 ♗g5 ♗e7
15 ♖f3 g6 16 ♘f6+ ♔c7 17 0-0-0
♘d7 18 ♕f4 ♘xf6 19 exf6+ ♗d6
20 ♕g4 ♖c8 21 ♖h3 ♖h5 22 ♘e2.
Yet I find it hard to believe 9 ...
hxg4 is good, as White may

continue (instead of 11 ♘h5?) **11
♘xe4** dxe4 12 ♕xe4 ♘f5 (what
else?) 13 ♗g5! and Black is in
dire straits. For example, after
13 ... ♕xd4? there follows 14
♕xd4 ♘xd4 15 0-0-0, while **13
... ♗e7** also fails after 14 0-0-0
♗xg5+ 15 hxg5 ♖xh3 16 ♗xh3
♕xg5+ 17 f4.

10   ♗g5   f6

Practically forced; if 10 ...
♕b6 11 a3! and now:

a) 11 ... ♗xc3+ 12 bxc3 hxg4 13
♘xe4! gxh3 14 ♘d6+ ♔f8 15
♖b1±; or

b) 11 ... hxg4 12 axb4! gxh3 13
dxc5±, according to Day.

11	♗d2	♗xc3
12	bxc3	♘c6
13	exf6	gxf6
14	♘xe4	dxe4
15	♕e2	*(36)*

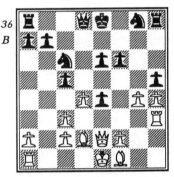

White's superiority is evident. He has two far-ranging
bishops and Black's central
pawn formation is loose. 15 ...
f5 16 gxf5 exf5 16 ♕c4! is very
unpleasant for Black, so he has
no choice but to sacrifice his
front e-pawn.

15   ...   ♕d7

16	♕xe4	0-0-0

Vasiukov adds a question mark to this move and proposes instead **16 ... hxg4** 17 ♕g6+ ♕f7 18 ♕xg4 0-0-0 as a better try. However I cannot see how Black defends after 19 ♗c4 f5 20 ♕e2 ♖e8 21 ♖e3 ♖xh4 22 0-0-0. In fact, the ugly **18 ... f5** might be the sole chance of holding on.

17	g5!

From now on White's game plays itself, as Black has no real counterplay on either flank.

17	...	♘ge7

In a bad position every move is bad and the same applies here, as on 17 ... f5 White's reply 18 ♕d3! (preparing to meet 18 ... ♘ge7 with 19 ♕c4) leaves no doubts about the final outcome. Black can hardly open up the position with 18 ... cxd4 or 18 ... e5, since in both cases his knights would be no match for the powerful white bishops.

18	gxf6	♘f5
19	♖d3	cxd4
20	cxd4	♖hg8
21	♗g5	♘b4
22	♖d2	♔b8
23	♖b1	♘d5
24	c4	

Preparing to double rooks on the b-line. Normally one would sacrifice material to achieve such a position, but here White is two pawns up!

24	...	♘b6

25	c5	♘d5
26	♖db2	♔a8
27	f7	♕xf7
28	♗xd8	♖xd8
29	♖xb7	♕f6

On 29 ... ♕xb7 there follows 30 ♖xb7 ♔xb7 31 ♕xe6 ♘xd4 32 ♗a6+ ♔a8 33 ♕f7, mating quickly.

30	♕d3	1-0

Black resigned as he cannot meet the threat of mate starting with 31 ♖xa7+.

Game 2
Minasian - Miles
Moscow GMA 1989

1 e4 c6 2 d4 d5 3 e5 ♗f5 4 ♘c3 e6 5 g4 ♗g6 6 ♘ge2

6	...	♗e7

This is Miles' pet line, with which he has suffered a number of reverses. Black wants to prevent h2-h4 even at the cost of impeding the development of his king's knight; in fact, Black hopes that he will be able to exploit the weak side of 6 g4 by ... h7-h5, after which his knight can be deployed to f5 via h6.

7	♗e3

Besides the game continuation, the following options are possible for White:

a) 7 ♘f4 c5 8 dxc5 d4 9 ♘xg6 hxg6 10 ♘e4 ♗xc5 11 ♘xc5 ♕d5 12 ♘xb7 ♕xh1 13 ♘d6+ ♔f8 with an unclear position in Nunn-Chandler, Wiesbaden 1981.

b) **7 ♗g2 ♘d7 8 0-0 h5 9
♘f4 hxg4 10 ♘xg6 fxg6 11
♕xg4 ♘f8 12 ♘e2 ♘h6 13 ♗xh6
♖xh6 14 b3 ♗a3 15 ♖ab1 a5 16 c4
♕h4 17 h3 ♕xg4 18 hxg4 g5∓ 19
f4 gxf4 20 ♘xf4 ♗e7 21 ♘h5
♖g6 22 ♖f4 ♗g5 23 ♖f3 ♗h6 24
♖bf1 ♘h7 25 cxd5 cxd5 26 ♘f4
♗xf4 27 ♖xf4 ♖c8 28 ♖1f2 ♖c1+
29 ♗f1 ♘g5 30 ♔g2 ♘d7 31 ♗b5+
♔c7 32 ♗d3 ♖h6 33 ♖c2+ ♖xc2+
34 ♗xc2 ♖h8 35 ♗g6 ♔d7 36 ♖f1
♖h6 37 ♗b1 ♖h4 38 ♔g3 ♖h3+
39 ♔f4 ♘f7 40 ♗g6 ♘d8 41 ♔g5
♖h8 42 ♗h5 ♔e7 43 ♔g6 ♖f8 44
♖c1 ♘c6 45 ♔xg7 ♖f4 46 g5
♖xd4 47 g6 ♘xe5 48 ♖c7+ ♔d6
49 ♖xb7 ♖d2 50 ♖b6+ ♔e7 51
♖b7+ ♔d6 52 ♔h6 ♘xg6 53
♗xg6 ♖xa2 54 ♗e8 e5 55 ♔g5
♖g2+ 56 ♔f5 ♖f2+ 57 ♔g4 e4 58
♖d7+ ♔e6 59 ♖d8 ♔e5 60 ♗c6
♖g2+** and ½-½ in van der Wiel-
Miles, Ter Apel 1987.

Nunn's **7 ♘f4** is logical and
clearly more testing than **7
♗g2**, but Minasian's move looks
more flexible than both these
alternatives.

c) **7 ♗h3!?** (a suggestion
from the author; the idea behind this weird-looking move
being to support the advance
f2-f4-f5) **7 ... h5** (critical but
risky; however after **7 ... ♗b4 8
♘g3** planning a2-a3 and 0-0
White keeps a slight advantage,
while **7 ... ♘d7 8 f4 ♗b4** {or **8 ...
♗h4 9 ♘g3** threatening f4-f5} **9
0-0 ♕h4 10 ♔g2 h5?! 11 g5! ♘e7
12 ♘g3** leaves the black queen
imprisoned in enemy territory)

8 ♘f4 hxg4 9 ♗xg4! ♗h7 (9
... ♗f5? **10 ♗xf5 exf5 11 e6±**) **10
♘xe6!?** (**10 ♖g1!?** is also interesting) **10 ... fxe6 11 ♗xe6
♗b4 12 ♕h5+! g6 13 ♕h3** (*37*)

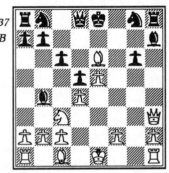

White's attack is more than
enough compensation for the
missing piece. Therefore, re-
searchers should turn their
attention to the continuation **11
... ♕h4!? 12 ♖g1!**, the consequences of which are unclear.

7	**...**	**♘d7**
8	**♕d2**	**h5**
9	**♘f4**	**hxg4**
10	**♘xg6**	**fxg6**
11	**♗d3**	

Another option here is **11 h3
♘f8 12 0-0-0 ♕a5 13 a3 b5 14
♘a2 ♕xd2+ 15 ♔xd2 a5 16 ♘c1
♔f7 17 ♘d3 ♖h4 18 ♗g2 ♘h6 19
hxg4 ♖xg4 20 ♗f3 ♖h4 21 ♖xh4
♗xh4 22 ♖h1 ♗e7 23 ♔e2 ♘f5 24
♗g4 b4 25 a4 ♘d7 26 ♖c1** from
Kamsky-Miles, New York 1989,
where White had good com-
pensation for the pawn but
probably not more than that,
despite the final outcome: **26 ...
♖h8 27 c3 b3 28 c4 ♘b6 29 cxd5
cxd5 30 ♖c7 ♖c8 31 ♖b7 ♘xa4**

32 ♗xf5 gxf5 33 ♗g5 ♖e8 34
♘d2 ♖c8 35 ♗xa5 g5 36 ♘b4
♖e8 37 ♘d6 ♔f8 38 ♖xb3 ♗xd6
39 exd6 ♖d8 40 ♖b4 ♘xb2 41
♖xb2 ♖xd6 42 ♖b8+ ♔e7 43
♖g8 g4 44 ♖g7+ ♔f6 45 ♖g8
♖a6 46 ♘e5 ♖a4 47 ♖g6+ ♔e7
48 ♔e3 f4+ 49 ♔d3 ♖a3+ 50
♔d2 ♖a4 51 ♔c3 g3 52 fxg3
fxg3 53 ♔d3 ♖a3+ 54 ♔e2 ♖b3
55 ♔f1 ♔f8 56 ♔g2 ♖b4 57 ♖g4
and 1–0.

> **11 ...   ♘f8**

Black's idea becomes apparent: this knight will defend
the weak pawns, enabling the
rest of his pieces to take up
important posts on the kingside (principally the other
knight on f5). Since the fight
usually revolves around the
mutual weaknesses existing
there, a successful blockade by
Black would automatically
grant him significant winning
chances. However, it is impossible to achieve these aims if
White plays energetically.

> **12 0-0-0**

Interesting is **12 ♘e2!?**
which deprives Black of the
option given in the next note.
Although this lets Black develop his knight to h6 without
the preliminary ... ♖h8–h4, this
might not be significant after
12 ... ♘h6 13 0-0-0 ♘f5 14 c4!?
when it's not clear how Black
can profit from the omission of
the rook move.

> **12 ...   ♖h4**

12 ... ♘h6? would be met by

13 ♖dg1 or 13 h3, with a clear
advantage for White in both
cases, for example, after 13 h3,
Zapolskis - Furdzik, Chrudim
1992 continued 13 ... gxh3 14
♖xh3 ♖g8 15 ♗xh6 gxh6 16 ♖g1
♔d7 17 ♖xh6 ♕e8 18 ♕f4 ♔c7 19
♘e2 (± Zapolskis).

However, in preparing ...
♘g8-h6, Miles misses a chance
to prevent the knight manoeuvre that follows. According
to Dokhoian, it was possible to
play **12 ... ♕a5!? 13 ♖dg1 ♖h4!**
with an unclear position, although even here Zapolskis' **13
♕e2** casts doubt on this assessment, e.g. 13 ... ♖h4 14 f3!
gxf3 15 ♕xf3 ♘h6 16 ♗f2 ♗g5+
17 ♔b1 ♖f4 18 ♕g2 ♕d8 19 ♘e2
♖g4 20 ♕f3 ♗e7 21 h3 ♖g5 22
♗e3 ♖f5 23 ♗xf5±, or 13 ... ♗b4
14 ♘d2 intending a3±.

> **13 ♘e2!±   ♘h6**
> **14 c4   ♘f5?**

Another Dokhoian sugges-
tion here is **14 ... ♕d7** 15 cxd5
cxd5 16 ♗g5 (16 ♕a5!?) 16 ...
♗xg5 17 ♕xg5 ♕e7 18 ♗xg6+
♔d7. After Miles' error, White
is winning.

> **15 ♘f4   ♔f7**
> **16 ♔b1   ♘d7**
> **17 cxd5   cxd5**
> **18 ♘g2   ♖h8**

It is evident that Black's
troops have become disorganized in the last few moves. The
fact that he has to play such
moves as 16 ... ♘d7 and 18 ...
♖h8 speaks fluently about the
failure of his strategy.

19	♕e2	♘h6
20	h3	gxh3 *(38)*

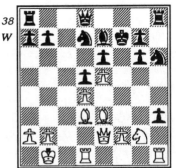

21	♗xg6+!?	♔xg6
22	♘f4+	♔f7
23	♕h5+	♔g8
24	♘xe6	♕e8?

A better defensive try was **24 ... ♕b6**. Black's congested pieces cannot provide their king with real protection.

25	♖dg1!+-	♗f8
26	♕xh3	♘f7
27	♕f5	♖c8
28	♖xh8+	♘xh8
29	♘xg7	♗xg7
30	♗h6	♖c1+
31	♔xc1	1-0

Game 3 ⅝³¹⁄⁹⁵

Kotronias – Sax
Burgas – Elenite 1992

1 e4 c6 2 d4 d5 3 e5 ♗f5 4 ♘c3 e6 5 g4 ♗g6 6 ♘ge2
   6 ... f6!? *(39)*

This is the main alternative to the most usual continuation 6 ... c5. Black provides his bishop with a retreat square on f7 while hitting White's central pawn wedge.

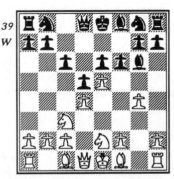

   7 h4

7 ♘f4 was supposed to be the main line but my research indicates that it's probably worse than 7 h4. Known to theory is 7 ... ♗f7 8 ♕e2!?, from Timman-Anand, Amsterdam 1992, which gave White an edge after 8 ... fxe5 9 ♕xe5 ♘d7 10 ♕e2 ♕e7 11 ♘d3 ♗g6 12 h4! (the position is much better for White, according to Timman) 12 ... ♗xd3 13 ♕xd3 e5 14 ♗g5 ♕f7 15 0-0-0 ♗d6 16 dxe5 (Timman considers this second-rate, suggesting 16 ♕g3!) 16 ... ♘xe5 17 ♕e2 ♕f3! 18 ♕xf3 (?! by Timman, who offers instead 18 ♕e1!? ♕xh1 19 ♖xd5! ♗c7!=) 18 ... ♘xf3 19 ♗e3 ♘h6 20 ♘e4 (?! again by Timman) 20 ... ♗e5 21 ♘g5 ♘xg5 22 hxg5 ♘xg4 23 ♗d3 g6 (now Black ought to win) 24 ♖de1 0-0 25 ♗c5 ♖fe8 26 ♖h4 b6 27 ♖xg4 bxc5 28 c3 ♖ab8? (the immediate 28 ... c5-c4 would have given Black a clear advantage) 29 ♔c2 c4 30 ♗xc4 dxc4 31 ♖ge4 ♖f8 32 ♖xe5 ♖xf2+ 33 ♖1e2 ♖xe2+ 34 ♖xe2 ♖b5 35 ♖g2 ♔f7 36 ♖g4 ♖c5 37

♔d2 ♔e6 38 ♔e3 ♖e5+ 39 ♔d4 ♖e2 40 ♔xc4 ♖xb2 41 a4 ♔f5 42 ♖g1 and ½–½.

The reason I did not choose this line against Sax is that Black can respond with 7 ... **fxe5!** and now:

a) **8 ♘xe6** ♕e7 9 ♘xf8 exd4+ 10 ♗e2 dxc3 11 ♘xg6 hxg6 (11 ... cxb2?! 12 ♕xb2 hxg6 13 ♕d4 led to an initiative for White in Efimov–Vdovin, USSR 1980) 12 ♕d3 ♘f6 13 ♕xc3 ♘bd7 14 ♗e3 ♘e4 was unclear in Nunn–Andersson, London 1982;

b) **8 ♘xg6** hxg6 9 dxe5 ♘d7 10 ♗f4 ♗c5 11 ♗d3 ♘e7 12 ♗g3 ♕c7 13 ♘a4 a5 14 ♕d2 b5?! (14 ... ♗b4! 15 c3 b5 16 cxb4 axb4! 17 ♘c3 bxc3 18 ♕xc3 ♖a4∓ van der Wiel) 15 ♘xc5 ♘xc5 16 ♕g5 ♖h6 17 ♕e3 ♘xd3+ 18 cxd3 c5 19 ♖c1 ♖c8 20 0–0 and ½–½ in Sax–Korchnoi, Tilburg 1989;

c) **8 dxe5** ♗f7 9 ♕e2 (9 h4 ♘d7 10 ♘d3 h5 11 ♗g5 ♕a5 12 ♗d2 ♕c7 is also unclear, Kinley–Friedmann, England 1980) 9 ... ♘d7! (risky is 9 ... c5 10 ♘cxd5! exd5 11 e6 ♗g6 12 ♘xg6 hxg6 13 ♕f3, Fabri–Carpati, corr. 1983, with White obtaining a strong initiative for the sacrificed material) 10 h4 ♕c7 11 ♘d3 h5! (the best, since after 11 ... c5 12 ♘xd5!? ♕c6 13 ♘3f4 0–0–0 {13 ... ♘e7 14 ♗g2 ♘xd5 15 ♗xd5 exd5 16 e6±} 14 ♖h3! exd5 15 e6 ♗xe6 {15 ... ♖e8 16 ♖e3} 16 ♕xe6 ♕xe6+ 17 ♘xe6 ♖e8 18 ♖e3 d4 19 ♖e2 White keeps a slight edge) gaining perfectly satis-

factory play, e. g. 12 g5 ♘e7 13 ♗h3 c5 14 ♗d2 a6 and White is running out of steam.

7   ...   fxe5!?

This is better than the immediate 7 ... ♘d7. The game Stavrev–Slavov, Bulgarian Ch (Pazardzhik) 1991, saw an interesting tactical struggle after 8 f4 h5 9 f5 ♗f7 10 ♘f4 fxe5 11 dxe5 ♘xe5 12 fxe6 ♗g6 13 ♘xg6 ♘xg6 14 gxh5 ♘e5 15 ♕e2 ♕f6 16 ♗g2 ♘c4 *(40)*

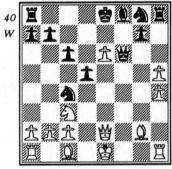

17 ♘xd5 cxd5 18 ♗xd5 ♗b4+ 19 c3 ♗xc3+ 20 bxc3 ♕xc3+ 21 ♔f1 ♘e7 22 ♗xc4 0–0+ (a rare instance of castling short with check!) 23 ♔g2 ♖ac8 24 ♗g5 ♖xc4 25 ♖ac1 ♖g4+ 26 ♕xg4 ♕b2+ 27 ♔h3 ♕a3+ 28 ♔g2 ♕xa2+ 29 ♔h3 ♕b3+ 30 ♔g2 ♕b2+ 31 ♔h3 ♕a3+ and ½–½. White was probably better in the complications, but nevertheless the move **8 h5** ought to be preferred as it secures an advantage without any particular risks. The game Marjanović–Skembris, Pucarevo Z 1987 continued 8 ... ♗f7 9 exf6! (less convincing is 9 f4 ♕b6 10 ♖h3

0-0-0 11 a3 c5 12 ♘a4 ♕a5+ 13 c3 ♕c7 14 ♘xc5 ♗xc5 15 dxc5 ♘xc5 16 ♘d4 ♔b8 17 ♗e3 a6 18 ♘b3 ♘d7 19 ♕d4 ♘e7 20 exf6 gxf6 21 ♕a7+ ♔c8 22.0-0-0 ♖hg8 with an unclear position in Moutousis-Nikolaidis, Greek Ch (Athens) 1988, although White's play could be improved, e.g. 17 ♘b5) 9 ... gxf6 10 f4 ♕c7 11 ♘g3 e5 12 ♗h3 exf4 13 ♘ge2 ♗d6 14 ♕d3 ♘e7 15 ♖f1 and White's prospects are clearly better; Marjanović went on to win after 15 ... f5 16 gxf5 ♘f6 17 ♗xf4 ♗xh5 18 ♕g3! 0-0-0 19 ♕h4 ♖hf8 20 ♗xd6 ♕xd6 21 ♘f4 ♖de8 22 ♔d2!.

Taking everything into account, transposing to the next chapter with 7 ... c5 may be best for Black.

8 h5 ♗f7
9 dxe5 ♗e7?

This move is out of place here. Normally e7 should be reserved for the development of the king's knight, therefore 9 ... ♗b4!?, played in Westerinen- Groszpeter, Copenhagen 1988, seems more logical. That game continued 10 ♗g2 ♘e7 11 f4 ♘d7 12 ♗d2 ♕c7 13 ♘d4 ♕b6 14 a3 ♗a5 15 ♘xe6 ♗xe6 16 b4 ♕d4 17 bxa5 0-0 18 ♖b1 ♖xf4∓, but it is obvious that White's play could be improved at several points. The main strategic problem is that White's bishop bites on granite when developed on g2, therefore I suggest the alternative plan 10

f4 ♘e7 11 a3 ♗a5 12 b4!? ♗b6 13 ♘d4 ♘d7 (13 ... a5 14 ♖b1; 13 ... ♗xd4!? is critical but very committal as Black is left with an atrocious bishop on f7) 14 ♘f3! h6 15 ♗d3 when the bishop eyes both flanks and is ready to assist various attacking schemes.

For **9 ... ♘d7**, see Game 4, Marjanović–Campora.

10 ♗g2

10 f4 is impossible on account of 10 ... ♗h4+, but White does not mind developing his bishop on g2 now since 9 ... ♗e7? has created a lot of traffic problems in Black's camp.

10 ... ♗h4?!

Sax's idea is to continue with ... ♘g8-h6, ... ♘b8-d7, putting pressure on both e5 and f2. However, this plan is too artificial to enjoy any chance of success.

11 ♕d2!

A simple refutation. The threat of g4-g5 prevents ... ♘g8-h6 and forces either 11 ... h6 or the bishop's retreat to e7. In both cases White has succeeded in rendering Black's plan impossible.

11 ... ♗e7

The bishop retreats empty-handed, Black's sole gain being the strange-looking position of White's queen. After 11 ... h6 White could continue in a way similar to the game.

12 ♕e3!±

Improving the position of

the queen and at the same time stopping ... c6–c5 (12 ... c5? 13 ♘xd5! exd5 14 e6). White already enjoys an undisputed advantage in view of his lead in development and the lack of harmony in Black's position.

| 12 | ... | ♘d7 |
| 13 | b3! | ♛a5 |

White's last move revealed his intention of following up with ♗c1–b2 and 0–0–0, thus discouraging Black from **13 ... ♘b6** 14 ♗b2 c5?! which would merely weaken d5. Better, however, was **13 ... ♛b6** 14 ♛g3 0–0–0 (14 ... d4?! 15 ♘e4 ♛a5+ 15 ♗d2 ♛xe5 16 f4 ♛c7 17 ♘xd4 only makes things worse), as Black would then have more fighting chances than in the actual game.

| 14 | ♗d2 | ♛c5 |
| 15 | ♘d4 | b5 *(41)* |

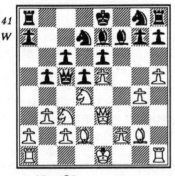

| 16 | f4 |

Setting in motion the pawn mass on the kingside. Unable to prevent the unpleasant threat of f4–f5, Black hurries to pin the knight on d4 in an effort to minimize its conse-quences.

16	...	♛b6
17	f5	♗c5
18	♘ce2	0–0–0
19	b4	♗xd4
20	♘xd4	♖e8
21	0–0–0	♘h6
22	♛c3!	

Not surprisingly, White's pressure has increased at a very fast pace. 22 ♛c3! creates numerous threats which can only be met by another forced move on Black's part.

22	...	♘xe5
23	fxe6	♗xe6
24	♘xe6	♖xe6
25	♗xd5	♖ee8?!

Slightly better was 25 ... ♖e7, although White would still be winning.

| 26 | g5 | ♘f5 |

After 26 ... ♘hg4 27 ♖hg1! the black knights would be tied up defending each other. In great time-trouble, the Hungarian Grandmaster and twice Candidate correctly tries to centralize as much as possible; however, his efforts do not have the desired effect in view of White's dominant bishops.

| 27 | ♗f4 | ♛c7 |
| 28 | ♗e4! | |

Not fearing 28 ... ♘d3+ 29 cxd3! with a winning position for White.

| 28 | ... | ♖hf8 |
| 29 | ♖hf1+– *(42)* | |

White has a dream position: both bishops point menacingly at Black's weakened queenside

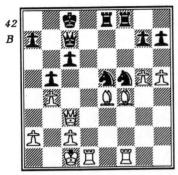

42
B

and his heavy pieces are also excellently placed, applying strong pressure on the open files; in contrast, Black's queen and rooks are tied to the defence of their cavalry, passively awaiting an inevitable loss of material.

29 ...   ♘d6!?

Trying to complicate the issue. 29 ... g6 is not better in view of 30 ♗h2! (Dorfman), and White has acquired the extra possibility of creating a dangerous passed pawn on the kingside after ♗e4xf5.

30 ♗d3!   ♘dc4

Despair, but Black had to lose something anyway.

31 ♗xc4   ♖xf4
32 ♖xf4   ♘xc4
33 ♖xc4

Getting rid of the annoying knight is the safest way to victory. Black's king is sufficiently exposed to succumb to the combined attack of White's forces.

33 ...   bxc4
34 ♕xc4   ♔b7
35 ♖f1?

But this is not the way to do it: thinking that 'everything wins', White falters in his opponent's time trouble. The prophylactic **35 ♔b1!** was called for, with an easily won game.

35 ...   ♖e7?

Sax is an excellent time-trouble player, but here he failed to notice my mistake as he had no more than ten seconds left. After **35 ... ♕e5!** 36 ♖f7+ ♖e7 (the move I completely overlooked; I thought 36 ... ♔b8 was forced when 37 ♕f4 is an easy win for White) 37 ♖xe7+ ♕xe7 38 ♕f4 White is better but not clearly winning in the ensuing queen ending.

36 ♖f5!

White doesn't have to be asked twice. Switching the rook onto the fifth rank was rather imperative on account of the ideas mentioned in the previous note.

36 ...   ♕d6
37 ♔b2   a6?
38 ♖a5

And Black's flag fell in this position. 37 ... a6? was a dreadful time-pressure error but Black's game was already beyond repair at that point.

1-0

Game 4
Marjanović – Campora
Nis 1985

1 e4 c6 2 d4 d5 3 e5 ♗f5 4

♘c3 e6 5 g4 ♗g6 6 ♘ge2 f6
7 h4 fxe5 8 h5 ♗f7 9 dxe5
    9   ...   ♘d7
    10 f4 *(43)*

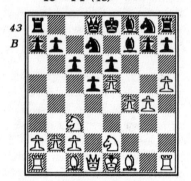

An important position for
the whole variation. Black has a
pawn preponderance in the
centre, White on the kingside.
This normally results in a lively
struggle with chances for both
sides.

    10   ...   ♕b6

Timman gives the move 10 ...
♕b6 an ! in his notes in *Informator 43* and Seirawan agrees
with him in his recent survey
book on the Caro Advance. The
alternatives are interesting, but
probably inferior:

a) The extravagant **10 ... g5**,
weakening the kingside and
also losing time, is thematic in
terms of destroying White's
central pawn chain (see van der
Wiel-Timman after White's 11th
move in the Main Game), but
more than Black's position can
handle at this moment when
development is far from complete. It is mentioned here only
because it led to a beautiful

game in Gazis-Makropoulos,
Greek Ch (Xilokastro) 1985,
where some typical dangers for
Black became blatantly obvious,
and also because it shows how
alert White must be in order to
take advantage of such mis-
takes in a typical sharp position
arising from the main line of
the Advance Variation: 11 hxg6
♗xg6 12 ♘d4 ♗f7 13 ♕d3 (preparing 0-0-0 and eyeing h7;
even stronger was 13 ♘f3
threatening ♘g5, but then the
following brilliancy would have
never seen the light of day) 13
... c5 14 ♘f3 c4 15 ♕e2 ♕b6 16
♗d2 ♕xb2 (practically forced
because of White's plan 0-0-0
followed by f4-f5, while 16 ...
d4 17 ♘xd4 ♕xd4 18 ♗e3 loses
right away) 17 ♖b1 ♕xc2 18 ♘d4
♕g6 19 ♖xb7! ♘c5 20 f5 exf5
(44)

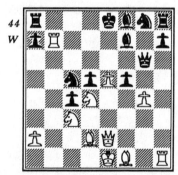

21 e6! (opening more lines and
threatening both 22 ♘xd5 and
23 ♕xc4) 21 ... ♗xe6 (the correct
reply to 21 ... ♘xb7 is not 22
exf7+♔xf7 when Black begins a
counter-attack with the threat
... ♖e8, but instead 22 ♘xd5!

with a powerful attack, e.g. 22 ... 0-0-0 23 ♕xc4+ ♗c5 {amusing is 23 ... ♔b8 24 ♘c6+ ♔a8 25 ♘c7#} 24 exf7 ♕xg4 25 ♗f4! threatening both ♗h3 and ♖h3 - analysis by Gazis) 22 ♘xd5! (forcing the capture of the rook, since 22 ... 0-0-0 is followed by 23 ♖c7+ and mate in two more moves) 22 ... ♘xb7 23 ♘xe6! (as usual, it would be wrong to recover material in the midst of the attack: after 23 ♘c7+ ♔f7 24 ♘xa8 the balance will eventually tip on the wrong side) 23 ... ♔d7 (23 ... ♔f7 24 ♘g5+ ♔g7 25 ♗c3+ is killing) 24 gxf5 ♕g3+ (not 24 ... ♕xf5 25 ♗h3 ♕b1+ 26 ♔f2 ♕xh1 27 ♘xf8++ and mate soon follows) 25 ♔d1 ♗d6 26 ♖h3 (adding more fuel to the fire) 26 ... ♕e5 27 ♕xc4 ♕xf5 28 ♖e3! (limiting the black king to the d-file) ♕b1+ 29 ♔e2 ♖c8 30 ♘f8+! ♗xf8 (Black has an unpleasant choice in severe time trouble: 30 ... ♔d8 31 ♕h4+ ♘e7 32 ♖xe7 or 30 ... ♖xf8 31 ♗h3+ ♖f5 32 ♘c3 are not much better) 31 ♗h3+ ♔d6 32 ♖e6+ ♔d7 33 ♕c8+! ♔xc8 34 ♖e8#.

b) **10 ... ♗c5 11 ♘d4 ♕b6** Black varied with 11 ... ♘h6 in the game Leuw-Groszpeter, Katerini 1992. After 12 ♗e3 ♕b6 13 ♘a4 ♕a5+ 14 c3 ♗e7 15 b4 ♕c7 16 ♗h3? g5! Groszpeter got a good position; instead of 16 ♗h3?, 16 ♗d3! was correct, when it is far from clear whether Black has achieved

anything positive with the paradoxical development of his knight on h6. The game ended: 17 0-0 ♖g8 18 f5 exf5 19 ♘xf5 ♘xf5 20 ♖xf5 ♗e6 21 ♗d4 ♗xf5 22 gxf5 g4 23 ♗g2 ♘xe5 24 ♗xe5 ♕xe5 25 ♕f1 ♕e3+ 26 ♕f2 ♕xf2+ 27 ♔xf2 ♖g5 and 0-1) **12 ♘a4 ♕a5 13 c3 ♗xd4 14 ♕xd4 c5 15 ♕d1±** Van der Wiel-Messa, Graz 1981. White is ready to answer 15 ... b5? with 16 ♘xc5! ♗xc5 17 b4; if Black avoids this, he simply prepares b2-b4, freeing the ♘a4 from its entanglement.

c) **10 ... c5!? 11 f5! ♘xe5 12 ♘f4** (12 fxe6!?) **12 ... exf5 13 ♕e2 ♗d6 14 ♘fxd5 ♕a5!** (The best move. After 14 ... ♘f6 15 ♗g5 White prepares castling long with a pleasant attacking position. But now Black's king will also find shelter on the queenside) **15 ♗f4 0-0-0 16 0-0-0 ♗xd5 17 ♗xe5!** (45) (If 17 ♖xd5? there follows 17 ... ♘d3+! 18 cxd3 ♗xf4+ 19 ♔c2 ♘f6∓)

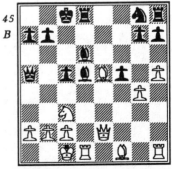

17 ... ♗xe5! (A well-considered decision. If 17 ... ♗xh1? 18 ♗xd6

♗c6 there follows 19 g5! with more than enough compensation for the exchange, e. g. 19 ... h6 20 ♕e6+ ♗d7 21 ♕e5 hxg5 22 ♖d5+−; better is 19 ... ♖e8 20 ♕f2 ♘e7 21 ♗xc5 with a strong initiative for White) **18 ♘xd5 ♖e8 19 ♕c4±** Kotronias-Skembris, Athens (2nd match game) 1987. After 19 ... fxg4 (19 ... ♘f6 20 ♖h3!?; 20 ♗g2±) 20 ♗g2 ♘e7 White should have continued with 21 c3 (21 h6!? is also interesting) 21 ... ♔b8 22 ♖hf1 obtaining a strong attack for the sacrificed material. It is well known that in such cases the presence of opposite-coloured bishops tends to favour the attacking side.

11 ♘d4!?

White's treatment of the opening is more in accordance with the strategy of the position than 11 ♗g2, played two years later in the game van der Wiel-Timman, Amsterdam 1987. That game ended 11 ... 0-0-0 12 b3 ♘e7 13 ♘a4 ♕c7 14 ♗e3 c5 15 c4 d4 (Black already has a slight advantage) 16 ♗f2 *(46)*

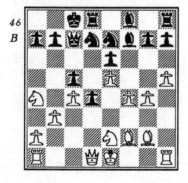

16 ... g5! (now this thrust is well timed, compared with the game Gazis-Makropoulos mentioned in the note after Black's tenth move) 17 hxg6 ♗xg6 18 ♘g3 ♘c6 19 0-0 ♗e7 20 a3 ♖hf8 21 ♗e1 d3?! (21 ... ♘dxe5 22 fxe5 ♘xe5∓) 22 ♘c3 ♘d4 23 ♘ge4? (23 ♖a2! is unclear) 23 ... ♗xe4 24 ♗xe4 ♘xe5 25 fxe5 ♖xf1+ 26 ♔xf1 ♘c2 27 ♔g1 ♘xa1 28 ♘b5 ♕xe5 29 ♗xb7+ ♔xb7 30 ♕f3+ ♔b6 31 ♗a5+ ♔xa5 32 ♕b7 ♕g3+ and 0-1.

11 ... 0-0-0

Instead **11 ... ♗c5** transposes to line "b" in the note to Black's tenth move.

12	**a3**	**c5**
13	**♘f3**	**♘e7**
14	**b4!**	**cxb4**
15	**axb4**	**♘c6**

15 ... ♕xb4 16 ♗d2 ♘c6 (16 ... ♕b6 17 ♖h3 ♘c6 18 ♖b1 ♗b4 {18 ... ♕c7 19 ♘b5 ♕b8 20 ♘bd4 or 18 ... ♘b4 19 ♘a2} 19 ♘b5±) 17 ♘g5 ♕e7 (17 ... ♗g8 18 ♘b5 ♕c5 19 ♖h3) 18 ♘b5 ♔b8 19 ♘d6 ♗g8 20 ♕b1 ♘b6 21 ♗b5 is a nightmare for Black.

16 ♘a4!

16 b5 is probably not as good. After 16 ... ♗b4! 17 ♗d2 ♗xc3 18 bxc6 bxc6 (Marjanović) there is no clear-cut way for White to get an advantage. The text forces Black to capture the b-pawn with his queen, giving White the necessary tempi to build up a dangerous attack.

16	**...**	**♕xb4+**

17 ♗d2   ♕e4+?!

More prudent was the passive **17 ... ♕e7**, but Campora probably disliked the position after 18 ♗b5 ♘db8 19 ♕b1 ♕c7 20 ♔e2!? when Black is kept under pressure and White's initiative fully compensates for the pawn minus.

18 ♔f2 *(47)*

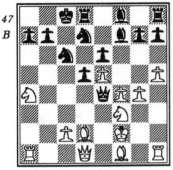

With the sacrifice of a pawn White has managed to open lines against the enemy king, thus acquiring a strong initiative. To add to Black's troubles, his queen is threatened with capture in the middle of the board and his bishop on f7 is completely out of play. Campora's next move averts immediate disaster, but at the heavy cost of a piece.

18 ...   ♘dxe5

No relief was offered by the alternative **18 ... ♘d4** 19 ♖h3 ♘xf3 20 ♖xf3 (± Marjanović). Even worse is **18 ... ♘c5?**, when 19 ♗b5! (threatening ♖h1-e1) ♘d4 20 ♘g5 forces immediate capitulation.

19 fxe5   ♘xe5

20 ♗d3!

A strong move, designed to do away with the only piece that could become a nuisance for White, namely Black's knight.

20 ...   ♘xd3+?

This is equivalent to resignation. Relatively best was **20 ... ♕xg4** 21 ♘xe5 ♕d4+ 22 ♗e3 ♕xe5, although Black cannot really hope to survive in view of his exposed king.

21 cxd3

Now White is completely winning since all the trumps are on his side: in addition to three open files on the queenside, he also controls the important h2-b8 diagonal leading directly to the black monarch.

21	...	♕xg4
22	♕c2+	♔b8
23	♖h4	♕f5
24	♘c5	♗xh5
25	♖xh5	

A problem-like mate could occur after **25 ♖f4 ♕h3 26 ♘a6+ ♔a8 27 ♘c7+ ♔b8 28 ♖xa7! ♔xa7 29 ♖a4+ ♔b6 30 ♗e3+ d4 31 ♗xd4+ ♖xd4 32 ♘a8+ ♔b5 33 ♘xd4#!** (Marjanović). However, the Yugoslav GM missed this elegant win in time trouble.

25	...	♕xh5
26	♘xb7!	♗e7
27	♘xd8?	

Time-pressure is responsible for the biggest blunders in tournament chess. This time White misses an easy mate with **27 ♗f4+ ♔a8 28 ♘xd8 ♖xd8 29 ♕c6#**. Fortunately for him the position is still won.

27	...	♗xd8
28	♗f4+	♔b7
29	♗e3	d4
30	♗xd4	♗b6
31	♕b2!	♕f7 (48)

There is no defence. On 31 ... ♖b8 32 ♗xb6 axb6 33 ♕xg7+ wins.

32 ♖xa7+! 1-0

Black resigned since on 32 ... ♔xa7 the sequel would be 33 ♕xb6+ ♔a8 34 ♕a6+ ♔b8 35 ♗e5+ with inevitable mate.

Conclusion

Games 3 and 4 show that the variation with 6 ... f6 offers both players a lot of interesting ideas. At present White's chances seem to be slightly better, but there is still room for investigation especially in the lines 'a' and 'c' after White's 10th. Black's problem is that the knight on d7 is not very well placed and this is perhaps a good argument for choosing 6 ... c5.

Main Line: 6 ... c5 7 h4, Without 7 ... h6 (Games 5-7)

Game 5
Nagel - Wouters
Corr. 1988

1 e4 c6 2 d4 d5 3 e5 ♗f5 4 ♘c3 e6 5 g4 ♗g6 6 ♘ge2

6	...	c5

The most thematic continuation, increasing Black's central influence while at the same time preparing to develop. The resulting positions are of a tactical nature and so a great deal of homework is required for those wishing to take up the 3 e5 variation. I hope that my coverage of this line will provide answers to all the key questions.

7 h4 (49)

The game Shabalov - Adianto, New York Open 1993 featured the move **7 ♗e3!?** which looks like a very playable deviation. Although Shabalov lost the game after several blunders I think that the opening was a success for him: 7 ... ♘c6 8 dxc5 ♘xe5 9 ♘f4 a6 10 ♕e2 ♘f6 11 0-0-0 ♗e7 12 ♗g2 ♘exg4 13 ♘fxd5! exd5 14 ♘xd5 ♘xd5 15 ♕xg4 0-0 16 ♗xd5±. This bears a close resemblance to Game 9, with which it should be compared carefully.

At this moment Black has to make a difficult decision: the insecure position of the bishop on g6 puts an abrupt end to

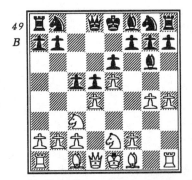

49
B

any thoughts about 'normal' development and a weakening move has to be made. It is by no means clear what is the best way to solve this dilemma but one point is clear: White's threat of h4-h5 cannot be ignored without serious consequences. After **7 ... ♘c6?!** **8 h5 ♗e4** White has two ways to prove the superiority of his position:

a) **9 ♘xe4!?** dxe4 10 c3 cxd4 11 ♘xd4 ♗c5 (11 ... ♘xe5 12 ♕a4+±; 11 ... ♘xd4 12 cxd4 ♗b4 13 ♗d2± Boleslavsky) 12 ♗e3 ♘xd4 (12 ... ♕b6!?) 13 ♕a4+!± Kengis-Kivlan, USSR 1979.

b) **9 ♖h3!** and Black's last move looks like a shot in empty space.

However, after completing this book, I had to defend my variation in the Caro Advance against a surprising novelty. In the game Kotronias-Djuric, Corfu 1993, after 7 ... ♘c6 8 h5, the Yugoslav GM, noted for his uncompromising play introduced the move **8 ... ♗xc2!?**. Although it's hard to believe

that such a move is objectively correct, I couldn't prove a clear advantage in the post-mortem. The game went 9 ♕xc2 cxd4 10 ♘b1 (on 10 ♘d1 White has to reckon with 10 ... ♖c8 11 ♗g2 ♕d7) 10 ... ♖c8 11 ♕a4 ♕b6 (11 ... ♕d7 is interesting, but probably inferior) 12 ♘f4 and now Djuric missed the best continuation **12 ... ♔d8!**. This move creates the dual threats of ... ♘xe5 and ... ♘b4 and after the logical 13 ♘a3 Black may (only now!) trade queens with 13 ... ♕b4+! 14 ♕xb4 ♗xb4+ when in comparison to the game he gets c4 for his knights by capturing on a3. The resulting endgame seems unclear to me, so this line holds good prospects for investigation by both sides in the near future.

Djuric's actual choice, **12 ... ♕b4+?!** immediately restores material equality by gaining a third pawn for his piece, but this proves inadequate as White is not saddled with any weaknesses and he may put to good use his bishop pair. The continuation was 13 ♕xb4 ♗xb4+ 14 ♔d1 ♘xe5 15 ♘d3! ♘xd3 16 ♗xd3 ♘f6 17 f3 h6?! (better 17 ... 0-0) 18 ♗f4 (threatening ♗e5) 18 ... ♘d7 19 ♘d2 ♔e7 20 ♘b3 e5 21 a3! ♗d6 22 ♖e1 (interesting is 22 ♗d3 intending ♘xd4) 22 ... ♔d8 23 ♗g3 ♖c6 24 ♘a5 ♖c7 25 ♔d2! ♖e8 26 ♖ac1 ♘f6? (26 ... ♘b6? 27 ♖xc7 ♔xc7 28 ♘b3+-; 26 ... ♔c8?! 27 ♗f5+-; 26 ... ♖e7)

27 ♘f5 ♖ee7?? (a terrible blunder, but his position was already lost) 28 ♘xb7! 1-0.

The alternatives that will be examined in the remaining games are 7 ... f6, 7 ... cxd4, 7 ... h5 and 7 ... h6.

7   ...   cxd4

The old main line, which became the subject of a long theoretical debate in the '80s after Seirawan won brilliantly with it against Hort at Bad Kissingen 1981. Its main advantage is that it weakens for ever the support of White's strong e5-pawn and thus discourages f4-f5, but on the other hand it helps the white knight approach the centre with gain of time and therefore considerably improves White's chances in the complications which follow.

Another option trying to improve on the 6 ... f6 variation is **7 ... f6**, planning to develop the queen's knight on c6 in order to exert more effective pressure on the centre. However, it has the corresponding disadvantage of loosening his own central structure and a likely continuation is **8 ♗g2!?** (now the bishop's development on g2 is more to the point - compare with Westerinen-Groszpeter in the notes to Game 3; Seirawan mentions only 8 ♘f4 and Nunn's 8 h5) **8 ... ♘c6 9 f4** (preparing f4-f5; White's minor pieces are ideally placed to exercise pressure on

d5 in case he successfully carries out the above-mentioned breakthrough) **9 ... ♘ge7** (possible is 9 ... fxe5, trying to stabilize the position in the centre, but after 10 dxe5 ♘ge7 11 ♘b5!? White keeps the initiative; the text, on the other hand, allows an interesting pawn sacrifice resulting in a lively game) 10 f5!? exf5 11 exf6 gxf6 12 g5! *(50)*.

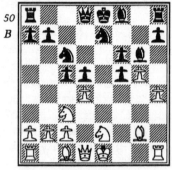

White has excellent dark-square compensation for the pawn, having vacated f4 for his knight and also preparing to bring his queen's bishop efficiently into the game. Although this is hardly the final word on 7 ... f6, I think that it is quite characteristic of what White should be aiming for in such positions.

8   ♘xd4   h5
9   f4!

This is a big improvement over Hort's **9 ♗b5+?!** in the aforementioned game. The continuation was 9 ... ♘d7 10 ♗g5 ♗e7 11 f4 hxg4 12 ♕xg4 ♗xg5! 13 fxg5 ♗h5 14 ♕h3 ♘e7

15 ♔d2 ♖c8 16 ♖ae1 ♕b6 17 ♘b3 a6 18 ♗xd7+ ♔xd7 19 ♔c1 ♖c4 20 ♘d2 ♖b4 21 a3?! ♖xb2!! 22 ♘a4 ♖xc2+ 23 ♔xc2 ♖c8+ 24 ♘c3 d4 25 ♖b1 ♕c6 26 ♖b3 ♘d5 27 ♘b1 ♗g4 28 ♕h2 dxc3 29 ♔c1 a5 30 ♖f1 ♗f5 31 a4 c2 32 ♘a3 ♕xa4 33 ♖xb7+ ♔c6 34 ♖xf5 and White at the same time resigned.

9   ...   hxg4

Wrong is **9 ... ♘e7?** 10 ♘cb5!±. **9 ... ♕d7!?** was tried in the 1986 correspondence game Korolev-Kastarnov; after **10 f5 exf5** the continuation was **11 gxf5 ♗xf5 12 ♘xf5 ♕xf5 13 ♕xd5 ♘c6 14 ♗h3 ♕xe5+ 15 ♕xe5+ ♘xe5 16 ♗f4 ♗d6 17 ♖d1 ♗b8 18 ♘d5** (Bouwmeester suggests 18 ♗c8!±, but this is not entirely clear in my opinion) **18 ... ♘e7 19 0-0 ♘7g6 20 ♗c8 a5 21 ♗e3 0-0 22 ♗xb7 ♖a7 23 ♗xa7 ♗xa7+ 24 ♔h1 ♖b8 25 ♗a6 ♖xb2 26 ♘f4 ♘xf4 27 ♖xf4 ♖xc2 28 ♖f5 f6 29 ♖xe5** and the game was agreed drawn. Instead, I believe, much stronger was **11 ♕e2!** , after which White enjoys a powerful initiative.

10   ♗b5+

In many positions arising after 6 ... c5, it is important to give this check when Black is unable to interpose with ... ♘b8-c6.

10   ...   ♘d7
11   f5

The most energetic continuation. Another possibility is 11 ♕xg4 ♘h6 12 ♕g2 ♕b6!? 13 ♗e3 0-0-0 14 h5 ♘h7 15 ♖h3! ♘c5 16 0-0-0 with a slight advantage for White in Nagel-Gebhardt, corr. 1989.

11   ...   ♖xh4 *(51)*

Also unsuccessful was Black's choice in Sax-Vadasz, Hungary 1984, which continued **11 ... ♗xf5 12 ♘xf5 exf5 13 ♕xd5 ♕c7** (13 ... a6 14 ♗g5 ♘e7 15 ♕xb7 axb5 16 ♘xb5±; 14 ... ♗e7? 15 ♗c4±) **14 ♗f4 ♘e7** (14 ... 0-0-0 15 ♕xf7) **and now 15 ♕d2!** 0-0-0 16 e6 ♘e5 17 ♗d7+ ♔b8 18 ♘b5 ♘f3+ 19 ♔d1 (Sax) would have won easily.

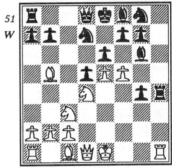

12   ♖f1!

After **12 0-0!?**, 12 ... ♖h1+! follows, with wild complications. The text is a big improvement over **12 ♖g1**, which was shown to be definitely inferior in the encounter van der Wiel-Speelman, Wijk aan Zee 1983: 12 ... ♗h5 13 fxe6 fxe6 14 ♘xe6 ♕b6 15 ♗xd7+ ♔xd7 16 ♕xd5+ ♗d6 17 ♘d4 ♖e8 18 e6+ ♔c8 19 ♗g5 ♘f6 20 ♕c4+ ♕c5 21 ♕xc5+ ♗xc5 22 ♗xh4 ♗xd4 23 ♖g3 ♖xe6+ 24 ♔f1 ♘e4 25 ♘xe4 and ½–½.

Another option is 12 ♗xd7+!?, attempting to force transposition to the game Moore–Mills analysed in the next note. This was White's choice in the game Krpelan–Durnik, Vienna 1991, which ended 12 ... ♔xd7 13 ♖f1 ♖h2 (13 ... ♖h5!?) 14 ♕xg4 exf5? (much better is 14 ... ♗h5! 15 fxe6 fxe6 and now 16 ♘xe6 ♔xe6 17 ♖xf8 {hoping for 17 ... ♕xf8 18 ♕xd5+ ♔e7 19 ♗g5+} 17 ... ♖h1+ does not work for White, but 16 ♕d3 offers an initiative for the sacrificed pawn; therefore this interesting continuation requires more practical tests) 15 ♘xf5 ♗xf5 16 ♕xf5+ ♔c6 17 ♗g5 ♗e7 18 ♗xe7 ♕xe7 (for 18 ... ♘xe7, see Moore–Mills immediately below) 19 0-0-0 ♘h6 20 ♕d3 ♕c5 21 ♘xd5 a5 22 ♕e4 ♔b5 23 ♖f3 ♔a6 and 1-0.

12   ...   exf5?!

This is a critical moment for the whole variation. The alternative **12 ... ♖h2?** led to a forced loss in the game Moore–Mills, USA 1984, after 13 ♗xd7+! (inferior is 13 ♕xg4!?, although after 13 ... ♗xf5? 14 ♘xf5 exf5 *(52)*

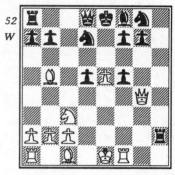

the typical breakthrough 15 e6! led to a win for White in Nunn–Wells, Chichester 1984; instead, 13 ... exf5 14 ♘xf5 ♗xf5 15 ♖xf5 ♕h4+ is only ±, according to Nunn) 13 ... ♔xd7 14 ♕xg4 exf5 15 ♘xf5 ♗xf5 (also losing is 15 ... ♗h5 16 ♕g3 ♖xc2 17 ♕h3

– analysis by Moore) 16 ♕xf5+ ♔c6 17 ♗g5 ♗e7 18 ♗xe7 ♘xe7 19 ♕f4 (another winning line provided by Moore is 19 ♕xf7 ♖xc2 20 ♕e6+ ♔c5 21 ♖d1) 19 ... ♕h8 (19 ... ♖xc2?? 20 ♕a4+) 20 ♕a4+ ♔c7 21 0-0-0 ♕h6+ 22 ♔b1 ♕c6 (22 ... ♕e6 23 ♘b5+ ♔c8 24 ♘d4+– Moore) 23 ♕f4 ♖h6 24 e6+ ♔b6 25 exf7 ♘g6 26 ♕b4+ ♔a6 27 ♕a3+ ♔b6 28 ♘xd5+ ♔b5 29 ♕d3+ ♔c5 30 ♕d4+ ♔b5 31 ♖f3 ♖h4 32 ♖b3+ ♔a5 33 ♕d2+ ♔a4 34 ♖a3+ ♔b5 35 ♖a5+ and 1-0.

Also bad is **12 ... ♗xf5** 13 ♘xf5 ♖h5 14 ♘xg7+ ♗xg7 15 ♕xg4 ♖xe5+ 16 ♔d1 ♔f8 17 ♖g1± (Nunn).

A dynamic way to continue fighting is Seirawan's suggestion of **12 ... ♖h5!?** which involves the sacrifice of a whole piece in order to wrest the initiative. The resulting positions are rich in tactical possibilities but for the time being there are no practical examples with this move. After **13 fxg6** Black has two options:

a) **13 ... ♖xe5+** 14 ♘ce2 ♕h4+

15 ♔d2 ♕g5+ 16 ♘f4; this looks better for White, as the white king will find shelter on the queenside after c2-c3, ♔d2-c2.

b) **13 ... ♕h4+** (Seirawan's intention) 14 ♔e2 ♖xe5+ (14 ... ♕h2+ 15 ♔d3!? ♖h3+ 16 ♗e3 ♕xe5 17 ♗xd7+ ♔xd7 18 ♖xf7+ is better for White) 15 ♗e3 is unclear. Black should avoid the tempting 15 ... f5? which is met strongly by 16 ♘xe6!; 15 ... 0-0-0 seems reasonable, but after 16 ♗xd7+ ♖xd7 17 ♖h1 Black has yet to prove that he has sufficient compensation.

13 e6!

An older suggestion was 13 ♗f4, tested in Westerinen-Adianto, Thessaloniki OL 1988. That game continued 13 ... a6 14 e6 (14 ♗a4 b5 15 ♘b3 ♖h3 16 ♗xd5 ♕h4+ 17 ♔d2 0-0-0 is unclear according to Adianto) 14 ... axb5 15 ♕e2 ♗e7 **16 exd7+?** ♕xd7 17 ♘dxb5 ♔f8 18 0-0-0 ♘f6 19 ♘c7 *(53)*

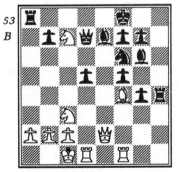

53
B

19 ... ♖a5 20 ♕e5 ♘h5 21 ♘7xd5 ♘xf4 22 ♕xf4 ♕d6 23 ♕c4 ♖c5 24 ♕a4 ♗g5+ 25 ♔b1 ♖c8 26 ♖fe1 g3 27 ♕b5 ♕c6 28 ♕e2

♔g8 29 ♕f3 f4 30 ♖e5 ♘h5 31 ♕e4 ♗xd1 32 ♖xg5 ♖e8 33 ♕d4 ♕h6 34 ♘f6+ ♔h8 35 ♘xe8 ♕xg5 36 ♕xd1 g2 37 ♘e2 ♖h1 38 ♘g1 ♕c5 and 0-1. Stronger seems Kamsky's **16 ♘xd5** ♘c5 17 ♘c7+ ♔f8 18 0-0-0 ♕c8 19 exf7 ♗xf7 20 ♘xa8 ♕xa8 21 ♘xf5 ♘e6 22 ♗g3! ♖h3 23 ♘xe7 ♔xe7 24 ♗d6+ ♔e8 25 ♕b5+-, but this has not yet been adopted in practice.

13	...	fxe6
14	♘xe6	♕e7
15	♕e2	♖h2!
16	♘c7+	*(54)*

Inferior is 16 ♕e5, played in the earlier game Kotliar-Retter, Israel 1986, which concluded 16 ... ♘gf6 17 ♗f4 ♖xc2 18 ♘c7+ ♔f7 19 ♕xe7+ ♗xe7 20 ♘xa8 ♖xb2 21 ♗xd7 ♘b4 22 ♗d2 ♘xd7 23 0-0-0 ♘a3 24 ♘b1 ♘c5 25 ♗e3 ♖e2+ 26 ♘xa3 ♖xe3 27 ♖xd5 ♖xa3 28 ♖xc5 ♖xa2 29 ♖c7+ ♔f6 30 ♖xb7 ♖a1+ 31 ♖b1 ♖xb1+ 32 ♔xb1 f4+ 33 ♔c1 f3 34 ♔d2 ♗e4 35 ♘c7 g3 36 ♔e3 ♔e5 37 ♖xf3 ♗xf3 38 ♔xf3 a5 39 ♘b5 and ½-½.

54
B

| 16 | ... | ♔d8?! |

A better defensive try is **16 ... ♔f7!**, as Black's king is a lot safer and may assist his army of pawns. I suspect this is also not enough in the long run, but it obviously demands a lot more precision on White's part to prove it.

17   ♕xe7+   ♗xe7
18   ♗f4   ♖xc2
19   ♘xa8   ♗h4+

The continuation **19 ... ♘c5 20 ♘xd5 a6? 21 ♗c7+ ♔c8 22 ♘(any)b6#** demonstrates the dangers faced by Black's king even after the exchange of queens. Also useless is **19 ... ♘gf6 20 ♖f2** etc.

20   ♔d1   ♖xb2
21   ♘c7   ♗f7
22   ♔c1   ♖f2

Black is forced to exchange his only rook, since 22 ... ♖b4 23 ♗d6 loses immediately.

23   ♖xf2   ♗xf2
24   ♘7xd5   g3
25   ♔c2

Black has kept four pawns for the rook, but his pieces are uncoordinated and the end is near. Still, White must not relax as the passed pawns may become dangerous at a moment's notice.

25   ...   ♘c5

25 ... g2 is premature: 26 ♗h2 g5 27 ♗g1 and White is winning easily after both 27 ... ♘h4 28 ♘e3 and 27 ... ♗g3 28 ♖d1!.

26   ♖d1   ♔c8
27   ♘e2   ♗h5

Thematic is 27 ... ♘e4 28

♘b6+! axb6 29 ♗d7+ ♔d8 30 ♗xf5+ etc.

28   ♘e3   ♗f3

Also losing are **28 ... a6** 29 ♖d5 ♗xe3 30 ♗xe3 ♘e4 31 ♗b6, **28 ... ♘f6** 29 ♘xf5 and **28 ... ♘e7** 29 ♖h1.

29   ♖f1   ♗xe2
30   ♗xe2   ♘e6 (55)

31   ♗xg3!   1-0

The final stroke. Black resigned, since both **31 ... ♗xg3 32 ♘xf5 ♗e5 33 ♗c4** and **31 ... ♗xe3 32 ♗c4 ♔d7 33 ♗xe6+ ♔xe6 34 ♖e1** are quite hopeless.

Conclusion

The variation with 7 ... cxd4 is perhaps the most complex sub-variation of the Caro Advance. At present White's chances seem better, but Seirawan's suggestion of 12 ... ♖h5!? might cause a renewal of interest in this discarded line.

Game 6
Van der Wiel - Icklicki
Brussels 1985

1 e4 c6 2 d4 d5 3 e5 ♗f5 4

♘c3 e6 5 g4 ♗g6 6 ♘ge2 c5
7 h4

    7   ...   h5!? *(56)*

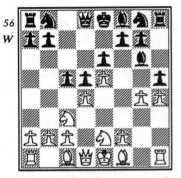

This idea has been consider-ed inadequate because of the game under examination, but my analysis indicates that if White relies on the game result without further analysis he may be confronted with a nasty experience. For example, in his recent book on the Caro Ad-vance Seirawan adopts estab-lished theory, reaching rather different conclusions from those which I suggest in the following analysis.

    8   ♘f4   ♗h7!

Strategically sounder than Seirawan's **8 ... ♘c6!?** which results in a deterioration of Black's pawn structure on the kingside and is examined ex-tensively in Game 7.

    9   ♘xh5

The Danish IM Klaus Berg has suggested here 9 g5!?; however this has never been tried in tournament practice.

    9   ...   cxd4
    10 ♕xd4   ♘c6

    11   ♗b5   ♘e7! *(57)*

An improvement on Bole-slavsky's recommendation of 11 ... ♗xc2?!, when 12 ♗g5 ♕d7 13 ♕d2 ♗h7 14 ♖c1± would follow. Black is in no hurry to restore material equality but opts instead for a flexible develop-ment of his pieces.

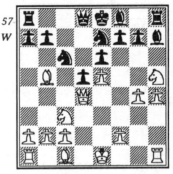

    12   ♗h6!

The only way to maintain the initiative. White develops with a gain of tempo, perceiving that the bishop on h6 will be im-mune from capture for several moves. White would have had big headaches after 12 ♗g5?! a6 13 ♗xc6+ ♘xc6 in view of Black's razor-like bishops.

    12   ...   ♕d7

According to my research, Black has a stronger move at this juncture:

12 ... a6!

This is a big improvement, since 13 ♗xc6+ ♘xc6 14 ♕f4 ♖g8! is only a slightly worse version of Black's position in the previous note. White has to be accurate now, therefore I present my analysis in some detail:

13 ♗xc6+ ♘xc6 14 ♕f4 ♖g8!

A novelty by the author. In-adequate is 14 ... gxh6?! (van der Wiel disposes of the alter-native 14 ... ♕b6 by 15 ♗xg7 ♕xb2 16 0-0±) 15 ♘f6+ ♔e7 16 ♘fxd5+! exd5 17 0-0-0! (worse is van der Wiel's 17 ♕f6+ as after 17 ... ♔e8 18 ♕xh8 {+- van der Wiel} 18 ... ♗xc2 the posi-tion is rather unclear) and Black has an unpleasant choice between:

1) 17 ... ♗g7 18 ♘xd5 ♔f8 19 e6±;

2) 17 ... ♔e6 18 ♖xd5±;

3) 17 ... d4 18 ♕f6+ ♔e8 19 ♕xh8 ♗g6 (19 ... ♗xc2 20 ♔xc2 ♕a5 {20 ... ♕c7 21 e6!} 21 ♘e4 ♘b4+ 22 ♔d2!± or 19 ... ♕a5 20 ♕xh7 dxc3 21 e6!+-) 20 e6! fxe6 (20 ... ♕a5 21 e7!) 21 ♖he1 ♗f7 (21 ... ♕xh4 22 ♖xe6+ ♔f7 23 ♖xg6! or 21 ... ♔f7 22 h5 ♕g5+ 23 f4! are both depressing for Black) 22 ♘e4 ♕a5 23 ♘d6+ ♔e7 24 ♘f5+ ♔e8 25 a3 with a strong initiative for White.

15 0-0-0 ♕a5! 16 ♖h3!

As in many lines so far, the rook transfer to the third rank combines defensive and attack-ing purposes. Here it is the only move, resulting in a highly complex position awaiting its first practical test. If 16 ... d4 17 ♖xd4! ♘xd4 18 ♕xd4±; or 16 ... ♘b4 17 ♖d4! ♖c8 (17 ... ♘xa2? 18 ♘xa2 ♕xa2 19 ♖a4+-; 17 ... ♘xc2 18 ♖a4 ♕c7 {18 ... ♕c5 19 ♖f3 ♗g6 20 ♗xg7 ♗xg7 21 ♘xg7+

♖xg7 22 h5 ♘h7 23 h6} 19 ♗xg7! ♗xg7 20 ♘b5 with a strong initiative; 17 ... ♘c6 18 ♖d2!?) 18 ♖xb4! ♕xb4 (18 ... ♗xb4 19 ♗xg7) 19 ♕xb4 ♗xb4 20 ♗xg7 and the white h-pawn will be valuable in the ending consid-ering that Black cannot effect-ively use his pressure on the c-file, e.g. 20 ... d4 (20 ... f5!? might be the only chance to complicate the issue) 21 ♘f6+ ♔d8 22 ♘xg8 dxc3 23 ♘f6 cxb2+ 24 ♔xb2; or 20 ... ♔e7 21 ♗f6+ ♔f8 22 ♗g5 and if 22 ... d4 23 ♘f6. However:

16 ... ♖c8! 17 ♖f3 ♗g6

leaves the position unclear and further tests are needed before a comprehensive evalua-tion is passed.

Nevertheless, Icklicki's move (if followed up correctly) also contains some drops of poison.

13 ♕f4 *(58)*

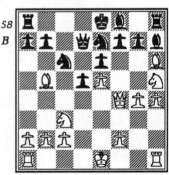

13 ... 0-0-0?

A decisive mistake. There was still time to mix things up by **13 ... ♘g6! 14 ♕a4! 0-0-0** with a difficult game for both sides. Inferior in this line would be 14 ♕g3?!, as after 14 ... 0-0-0 15 ♗xg7 (15 ♗g5?! ♘gxe5! 16 ♗xd8 ♕xd8 is better for Black) 15 ... ♗xg7 16 ♘xg7 ♘gxe5 Black gets excellent counter-play in the centre in return for the sacrificed pawn.

14 ♗xg7 ♗xg7
15 ♘xg7 ♘g6
16 ♗xc6!

Now it is clear why Black should have played ... ♘e7-g6 earlier. Since there is no piece hanging on h6, White hastens to exchange one of the dangerous knights and occupy d4 with his queen.

16 ... ♕xc6?!

More practical chances were offered by **16 ... ♘xf4 17 ♗xd7+ ♖xd7!** (on 17 ... ♔xd7 there follows 18 ♘e2! ♗e4 19 f3! ♗xf3 20 ♖f1!±) as White has to play very accurately to capital-ize on his advantage:

a) **18 ♘e2?! ♗e4! 19 ♘xf4?! ♗xh1 20 h5 ♖c7!** and White is in difficulties;

b) **18 ♘h5! ♘xh5 19 gxh5 ♖c7!?** (19 ... ♗e4! is tougher, when White still has some technical difficulties to over-come):

b1) **20 0-0-0?! ♖c4** with strong counterplay for Black;

b2) **20 ♖c1!: 20 ... ♖c4 21 ♘b5! ♖e4+ 22 ♔d2 ♖xe5? 23 ♘d6+ ♔d7 24 ♘xf7+–; 20 ... a6 21 ♘e2! ♗e4 22 ♖h2 ♖xh5 23 ♘g3!±** since 23 ... ♖xe5? fails to 24 f4!, trapping the rook in broad daylight.

17 ♕d4 ♘xe5

Black is two pawns down without any compensation. With his last move he hopes for a tactical *mêlée*, but White finds a neat way to finish him off.

18 ♕xe5 d4 (59)

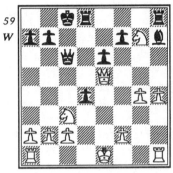

19 ♖h3!

The game is over. In addition to his extra piece, White soon gets a mating attack.

19	...	♕g2
20	0-0-0	♕xf2
21	♕c5+	♔b8
22	♘b5	♖d5
23	♕xa7+	♔c8
24	♕a8+	1-0

Game 7
Timman – Seirawan
Hilversum (4th Match Game) 1990

1 e4 c6 2 d4 d5 3 e5 ♗f5 4 ♘c3 e6 5 g4 ♗g6 6 ♘ge2 c5 7 h4 h5!?
8 ♘f4
8 ... ♘c6!? (60)

In matches of this calibre novelties like 8 ... ♘c6 are a bit

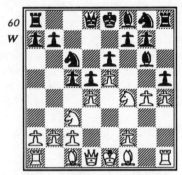

unusual; Black not only surrenders a powerful bishop, but also allows the crippling of his pawn structure for the sake of quick development and central pressure. Yet, although such moves are hardly aesthetically pleasing, this one is by no means easy to refute.

9   ♘xg6

White must take his chance while it is there, destroying the defensive pawn skeleton around Black's king. The game Tzoumbas-Kourkounakis, Athens 1992, saw the routine development **9 ♗b5** which resulted in a catastrophe for White: 9 ... ♘e7 (a move that would normally be met by ♘b5; it now secures complete control of f5 without any structural concessions while at the same time the destruction of White's pawn centre is assured) 10 ♗e3 hxg4 11 dxc5 ♗f5 and Black already had a strategically winning position due to the pressure on the weak white pawns and the tactical possibility ... g7–g5.

9   ...   fxg6

10   ♕d3?

A grave error which is already an indication that White has been taken by surprise. A logical explanation could be that Timman wanted to punish his opponent for the 'ugly' 8 ... ♘c6 as quickly as possible, but now the position is already lost!

White's best is Seirawan's suggestion to redeploy the remaining knight by **10 ♘e2!**, threatening both to increase the pressure on the weakened black kingside pawns and to stabilize White's central pawn chain with c2–c3. Black has nothing better than **10 ... cxd4** (10 ... hxg4?! 11 ♘f4 ♘xd4 12 ♕g4 ♖xh4? 13 ♗b5+!+- or 12 ... g5 13 ♘g6 {according to analysis by Greek masters, 13 ♘xe6 fails because of 13 ... ♕c8 – but not 13 ... ♕d7 because then follows 14 ♕xd4 cd4 15 ♗b5 with much the better ending for White} 13 ... ♘h6 14 ♕h5 ♕a5+ 15 ♗d2 ♕a4 16 ♘xh8+±) **11 ♘xd4 ♘xd4 12 ♕xd4 ♘e7**, reaching a position which the American Grandmaster considers satisfactory for Black. I disagree with this evaluation since after **13 ♗d3 ♘c6 14 ♕a4!** (worse would be 14 ♗xg6+? ♔d7 15 ♕a4 hxg4! which merely drives the black king to a safer spot, while also interesting in this line is 15 ... ♕b6!? 16 gxh5 ♗c5 17 ♖f1 ♖af8 as in Forster-Lyrberg, Guarapuava 1991, which concluded 18 f4 ♗e7 19 ♔e2 ♔c7 20 c3 ♘xe5 21 fxe5 ♖xf1 22 ♔xf1 ♖f8+ 23 ♔e2 ♕f2+ 24 ♔d1 ♕g2 25 ♗d2 ♖f1+ 26 ♔c2 ♖xa1 27 ♕e8 ♗c5 28 ♕f7+ ♔b6 29 ♕xe6+ ♔c7 30 ♕f7+ ♔b6 31 ♕e6+ and ½-½) **14 ... hxg4 15 ♗d2!** (White must avoid the queen exchange at all costs as after 15 ♗e3? ♕a5+! Black would have everything going his way) **15 ... ♖xh4 16 0-0-0 ♖xh1** (16 ... ♔d7!? – Kourkounakis) **17 ♖xh1 ♕b6 18 ♕xg4!**. Black dare not play 18 ... ♘xe5? in view of 19 ♗b5+!. Therefore **18 ... ♔d7** is forced, leaving White with much the better game after **19 f4**.

Editor's note: the latest word on 10 ♘e2 comes from the game Timman-Karpov, Djakarta Wch (17) 1993. There Karpov replied **10 ... ♘ge7!?** which led to great complications: 11 ♘f4 cxd4 12 ♗h3 (12 ♘xe6 ♕d7 13 ♘xf8 ♖xf8 eases Black's task) 12 ... ♘xe5 13 ♕e2 (13 ♘xe6 is met by 13 ... ♕a5+ 14 ♗d2 ♕b6, and 13 gxh5 by 13 ... ♘f5) 13 ... ♘7c6 (13 ... hxg4 14 ♕xe5 gxh3 15 ♘xe6 ♘c6 16 ♕e2!) 14 ♘xe6 ♕a5+ 15 ♔f1 hxg4 16 ♗xg4 ♗d6 17 ♔g2 ♕a6 18 ♕d1 ♘xg4 19 ♕xg4 ♘e5 20 ♕xd4 ♕c4 21 ♕xc4 dxc4 22 ♗e3 (Adianto pointed out that 22 ♗f4! ♔d7 23 ♘g5 {and not 23 ♘xg7 ♘f7!} 23 ... ♖ae8 24 ♖ad1 ♔c6 25 ♖he1 ♖hf8 26 ♖d4! followed by ♖de4 is probably winning for White) 22 ... ♔d7 23 ♘g5 ♗e7? (23 ... ♔c6) 24 ♖ad1+ ♔c6. Here

the commentators, including Seirawan who was acting as Timman's second, felt that **25 ♖d4** should give White good chances, e.g. 25 ... b5 26 ♖hd1 ♖ad8 27 ♘e6 or 25 ... ♗f6 26 ♖e1!. Instead a draw was agreed in the game following the moves **25 ♘e6 ♗f6 26 ♘d4+ ♔b6 27 ♘f3+ ♔c6 28 ♘d4+ ♔b6 29 ♖he1 ♖ae8 30 ♘e6+ ♔c6 31 ♘d4+ ♔b6 32 ♗g5 ♘f7 33 ♗e3 ♔a6 ½-½**.

10 ... cxd4!
11 ♘b5

Bad is 11 ♕xg6+? as the queen gets trapped after 11 ... ♔d7 12 ♘b5 ♘xe5. Note that Black would react in a similar way to 10 ♗d3.

11 ... hxg4!

A typical reaction, both in order to open the h-file and challenge control of the important outpost f5.

12 ♕xg6+ ♔d7
13 ♕xg4 ♕b6!

White has re-established material equality, but his position looks completely disorganized due to lack of central control. With his next move Timman tries to restore the coordination of his pieces by bringing the knight back into play, even at the cost of a pawn.

14 c3! dxc3
15 ♘xc3 ♘h6! *(61)*

Also good is 15 ... ♕d4! (Timman). The text move, although objectively correct, allows White to stir up some colourful complications.

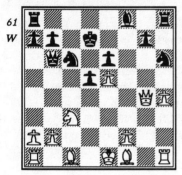

16   ♗xh6   ♛xb2
17   ♗d2!

Sacrificing the exchange to prevent Black from consolidating his advantage. In this way, White keeps some swindling chances alive.

17   ...   ♛xa1+
18   ♔e2   ♛b2?

Not only missing a picturesque win but also letting White back into the game. Seirawan himself points out the following winning line in *Inside Chess*: 18 ... d4! 19 ♗g2 d3+! 20 ♔e3 ♗c5+ 21 ♔e4 ♛b2 22 ♛xg7+ ♘e7! 23 ♖b1 (23 ♔xd3 ♖ad8-+) 23 ... ♛xd2 24 ♖xb7+ ♔c6 25 ♖xe7 (unfortunately for White he cannot discover an attack on the black king since all king moves - except 25 ♔f3 - are illegal) 25 ... ♖xh4+ 26 ♔f3 ♛xf2♯.

19   ♗h3

Of course, White cannot play 19 ♘xd5 ♛b5+.

19   ...   ♖e8
20   ♖b1   ♛c2

21   ♖xb7+   ♔c8
22   ♛b1?

White returns the compliment. After 22 ♖b5 g5! 23 h5 ♖h7 24 ♖xd5 ♔c7 the position is still unclear, according to Seirawan.

22   ...   ♗a3!-+

The game is decided. White probably overlooked that on 23 ♛xg7 Black answers 23 ... ♖h7!, repulsing all threats before continuing with his own attack.

23   ♖d1   ♗b2
24   ♘b5   ♔b8
25   ♘d6   ♘d4+
26   ♔e3   *(62)*

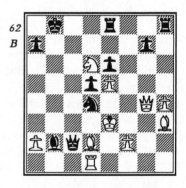

26   ...   ♖xh4!
27   ♛xh4   ♛xd1
28   ♗g4   ♘c2+
29   ♔d3   ♘e1+
         0-1

White loses his queen after 30 ♔e3 ♘g2+ 31 ♔d3 ♛b1+.

This game, in conjuction with its partner from the same match (Game 10), demonstrates how difficult it is to handle an innovation in this variation even at the highest level.

Main Line:
6 ... c5 7 h4 h6 (Games 8–11)

Game 8
Kotronias – Campora
Moscow 1989

1 e4 c6 2 d4 d5 3 e5 ♗f5 4 ♘c3 e6 5 g4 ♗g6 6 ♘ge2 c5 7 h4

7   ...   h6 *(63)*

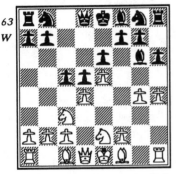

A modest choice, which has become more and more popular recently. We have already witnessed that the alternative choices are also interesting, yet the general impression remains that it is difficult to neutralize White's initiative within the limits of the existing theoretical knowledge. Therefore, to give preference to 7 ... h6!? is not a matter of taste, but rather a well-grounded decision to opt for a sound middlegame.

8   h5?!

White should refrain from an early h4-h5, as it deprives him of a later tempo-gain on Black's bishop when the f-pawn is advanced. The shortcomings of **8 h5?!** will become apparent in the following notes as well as in Nunn-Seirawan, Lugano 1983, featured in Game 10, Timman-Seirawan.

Another option is **8 ♘f4 ♗h7 9 ♗e3 ♘c6** (Black obtained an equal game after 9 ... ♘e7 10 dxc5 ♘ec6 11 ♗b5 ♘d7 12 ♕e2 ♕c7 13.0-0 ♕xe5 14 ♖ad1 ♕xc5 15 ♘fxd5 in Korchnoi-Byvshev, USSR 1951) 10 ♖h3 ♕b6 11 ♘a4 ♕a5+ with great complications, Papatheodorou - Kourkounakis, Athens 1992, but best is **8 ♗e3!**, as will be seen in the three remaining games of this chapter.

8   ...   ♗h7
9   ♗e3   ♕b6

Also good is **9 ... ♘c6**, which is likely to transpose after 10 ♕d2 and retains independent significance only after the try 10 dxc5, which proved unsuccessful in Yudasin-Seirawan, Jacksonville 1990: 10 ... ♘xe5 11 ♘d4 ♘f6 12 ♗b5+ ♘fd7 13 f4 a6! (Black has satisfactory development, therefore any tactical skirmishes taking place on his side of the board are likely to end in his favour) 14 fxe5 (14 ♗a4 ♘c4) 14 ... axb5 15 ♘dxb5 ♘xc5 16 ♕d4 ♘e4 17 ♕b6 ♕xb6 18 ♗xb6 ♔d7 19 0-0 f6 20 ♗d4 ♗e7 21 ♖ae1 ♖hf8 22 ♘xe4 ♗xe4 23 a3 ♗xc2 24 ♖c1 ♖ac8 25 exf6 gxf6 26 ♖f2 ♗d3 27 ♘c3 ♖c4 and 0-1.

10   ♕d2   c4

After 10 ... ♕xb2? 11 ♖b1

♕xc2 12 ♕xc2 ♗xc2 13 ♖xb7 c4 14 ♘b5 ♘a6 15 ♗g2 White has more than enough compensation for the pawn, according to analysis by Karpov and Zaitsev.

11	0-0-0	♘c6
12	f4	0-0-0

12 ... ♕a5 transposes to Nunn-Seirawan (see the note to White's 9th move in Game 10).

13   ♗h3!?

White's plan is to destroy Black's defensive formation by advancing the g-pawn all the way up to g6.

13   ...   ♔b8?

This loss of tempo allows White's inaccuracy on the 8th move to go unpunished. Correct is either **13 ... ♕a6!** or **13 ... ♘ge7!** with a slight advantage for Black.

14   f5   ♗b4?

The decisive mistake from a strategic point of view. When I saw this move on the board I was very relieved, since it self-blocks Black's attack (for the correct approach see Game 10, Timman - Seirawan). Much better was **14 ... ♕a6**, still with an unclear position.

15	a3	♗a5
16	♘f4	♖e8
17	♖hf1	

Now White's advantage is evident: more space, better development and the lack of an active plan for his opponent guarantee a long-term superiority. The only problem is how to increase the pressure in the most effective way, but since White can afford to take his time he will first attempt to exchange the black-squared bishops and thus create more weaknesses in the black camp.

17   ...   ♘d8

The fact that Black is forced to play such moves just to complete his development speaks volumes about his predicament.

18	♕e1!	♘e7
19	♗d2	♕c6
20	♘ce2	♗xd2+
21	♕xd2	

The first exchange of wood does nothing to relieve Black from his congestion. Meanwhile, the white pawn on f5 may never be taken because of the weakness of its counterpart on d5.

21   ...   ♘c8

22   ♕b4!

White's intention is to exchange queens, a highly favourable event because it will allow him to open another front on the queenside. Black's lack of space will then make it difficult for him to block all entrances to his side of the board.

22   ...   b6

23   ♘c3

Now the idea is to bring additional pressure on the d5-pawn by ♗h3-g2.

23   ...   a6?!

Better was **23 ... a5** immediately, but it could not have saved Black's head in the long run.

24 ♗g2   a5

Now the only move to keep his head above the water, because of the threat 25 ♘fxd5 exd5 26 ♗xd5 and in addition to the three pawns for the piece White will obtain a strong attack.

25 ♕b5   ♘e7
26 ♕xc6   ♘exc6 *(64)*

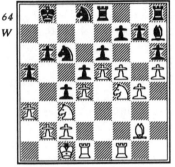

Now White may proceed slowly with preparation of the breakthrough b3 and attempt to infiltrate through the c- and f-files, as well as the knight jump to d6 via b5. However, the plan chosen in the game is far more typical of such positions, emphasizing the long-term space superiority provided by the central white pawns in the Caro Advance.

27 ♘fxd5!   exd5
28 ♗xd5   ♖hf8
29 ♗xc4

White has not sacrificed anything from the material point of view, while the h7-bishop is destined to remain a spectator (or worse) in the

coming stages of the battle. In addition, the black knights have no supported strongpoints from which to exercise their power while the black rooks lack open files. Meanwhile, White's central pawn roller will advance without facing serious resistance.

29 ...   ♘a7
30 ♖fe1!   ♘dc6
31 ♘b5!

Exchanges will emphasize White's advantage and free the way for the pawns. Black is so cramped that he does not have any real choice.

31 ...   ♘xb5
32 ♗xb5   ♔b7
33 ♖e3!   ♖d8
34 d5   ♘a7
35 ♗e2   ♖fe8
36 d6   ♗g8
37 b4!

Now focusing on the weak position of the black king, White opens more lines.

37 ...   axb4
38 axb4   b5
39 ♔b2   ♔b6
40 ♗f3   ♖d7
41 ♖a1

Setting a trap into which Black walks unsuspectingly. However, his position was already hopeless in view of the threat 42 ♖ea3.

41 ...   ♘c6? *(65)*
42 ♖a6+!   ♔xa6
43 ♗xc6   ♖ed8

Also useless was 43 ... ♖dd8 44 ♗xe8 ♖xe8 45 d7 ♖d8 46 e6

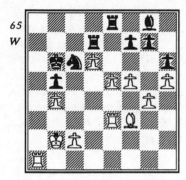

65
W

etc.

44 ♖a3+   1-0

The move order is important, since the black king may not go to b7 and after 44 ... ♔b6 45 ♗xd7 ♖xd7 46 ♖a8 ♗h7 47 ♖h8 the poor bishop is trapped inside the cage created by the white pawns.

Game 9
Timman – Karpov
Belfort 1988

1 e4 c6 2 d4 d5 3 e5 ♗f5 4 ♘c3 e6 5 g4 ♗g6 6 ♘ge2 c5 7 h4 h6
8   ♗e3! *(66)*

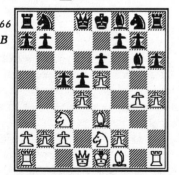

66
B

There are two main alternatives for Black: 8 ... ♕b6! (Game

10) and 8 ... cxd4 (Game 11). As we shall see, the most accurate move is 8 ... ♕b6!, overprotecting Black's c-pawn and preparing queenside castling. Karpov's choice 8 ... ♘c6 looks like a solid developing move, but Timman's treatment of the opening reveals its dark side.

8   ...   ♘c6?!
9   dxc5!

This move was first introduced in this game. White gives up the centre for tactical reasons, estimating that his lead in development will be of considerable help in the complications that will follow. In the rapid chess game Palamidas-Kourkounakis, Athens 1991, White committed the typical mistake of advancing immediately **9 h5** and the loss of time showed after 9 ... ♗h7 10 f4 ♕a5 11 ♕d2 ♖c8 12 f5 exf5 13 ♘xd5 ♕xd2+ 14 ♔xd2 fxg4 15 ♗g2 ♘ge7 16 ♖hf1 ♘f5 17 c3 ♘h4 18 ♗h1 ♘f3+ 19 ♗xf3 gxf3 20 ♘g3 cxd4 21 ♘xd4 ♖d8 22 ♘c7+ ♔d7 23 ♘b5 a6 24 ♘d6 ♗xd6 25 exd6 ♘xd4 26 cxd4 ♖c8 27 ♖xf3 ♖c2+ and Black won easily.

9   ...   ♘xe5
10   ♘f4!   a6?!

On **10 ... ♗h7**, best is 11 ♗b5+ ♘c6 12 ♕e2 with an initiative due to the enormous pressure White acquires on all open lines (ideas based on ♘xd5 are especially appealing). However, this line represented the lesser evil for Black. The dangers inherent in Black's position were shown in Kotronias-Theoharis, Athens (simul) 1992: after **11 ♕e2!?** (slightly worse than 11 ♗b5+) 11 ... ♘e7 12 0-0-0 ♕a5 13 ♖d4!? ♘c4?! 14 ♖xc4 dxc4 15 ♕xc4 0-0-0 16 ♗g2 ♘c6 White had a winning continuation in 17 ♘xe6! (Kourkounakis) 17 ... fxe6 18 ♕xe6+, e.g. 18 ... ♔b8 19 ♗f4+ ♔a8 20 ♕xc6!! or 18 ... ♖d7 19 ♖d1 ♕d8 20 ♗xc6 bxc6 21 ♕xc6+ ♕c7 22 ♕a8+ etc. This variation is not forced, of course, but the general impression is that White should be able to obtain an advantage no matter how Black plays.

Another possibility is **10 ... d4**, but according to Timman it will prove insufficient after 11 ♗b5+ ♔e7 12 ♘xg6+ (12 ♘fd5+!? exd5 13 ♗xd4 is also interesting) 12 ... fxg6 13 ♗f4 dxc3 14 ♗xe5±. The fact that Karpov judges it necessary to resort to a move like 10 ... a6 when behind in development speaks volumes about the state of Black's game at this point.

11 ♗g2 ♘f6
12 ♕e2!

A typical reaction, preparing queenside castling while adding pressure on the e-file. It is quite uncharacteristic of Karpov to get in such a horrible mess after only a dozen moves in the opening, therefore this example serves to emphasize the virulence of the Advance Variation

even against the very best opposition.

Note the similarity of this position to Shabalov – Adianto in the note to White's 7th move in Game 5, where White forewent the h-pawn advance.

12 ... ♘fxg4
13 ♗d4± ♗e4 (67)

67
W

Black is already in a very unpleasant situation. After the simple **14 ♘xe4 dxe4 15 ♕xe4** the ex-World Champion would have found it hard to put up a respectable defence. Consider the following variations (analysis by Timman):

a) **15 ... f5** 16 ♕xb7 ♕xd4 17 ♗c6++–;

b) **15 ... ♘c6** 16 0-0-0 ♘f6 17 ♗xf6 ♕xf6 18 ♕xc6+!+–;

c) **15 ... ♕a5+** 16 b4! ♕xb4+ 17 c3 ♕c4 18 ♕xb7 ♖d8 19 ♗f1! ♕a4 20 ♗xa6+–.

The move Timman chose, on the other hand, allows Karpov to display the iron determination for which he is famous, by performing yet another defensive miracle.

14 ♗xe4?! dxe4

15	0-0-0	♛c7
16	♝xe5	♞xe5
17	♞xe4	(68)

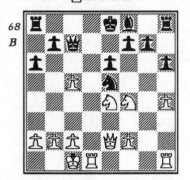

Despite his error on the 14th move, White still keeps a tremendous pull mainly due to his beautifully centralized knights. Black cannot grab a pawn by 17 ... ♝xc5? as he would be swiftly punished by 18 ♞xc5 ♛xc5 19 ♜he1 ♜c8 20 c3 ♞(any) 21 ♞xe6! (Timman). In this precarious situation, the ex-World Champion sticks to the only correct idea, trying to relieve his position by exchanges.

17	...	♜d8
18	♞h5!	

Tying the black bishop to the defence of the sensitive point g7 while preparing f2-f4-f5. Wrong would have been 18 ♜xd8+? ♚xd8! when the black king escapes to the queenside.

18	...	♞c6
19	f4?	

A hasty decision which throws away White's advantage. Before going on with his plan, White should "squelch" any counterplay Black might have and the most appropriate way to do so is by playing **19 c3!**. Black then has a sad choice between:

a) **19 ... g6** 20 ♞ef6+! ♚e7 21 ♜d6! ♜xd6 (21 ... gxh5? 22 ♞d5+-) 22 cxd6+ ♛xd6 23 ♜d1±;

b) **19 ... ♛e5?** (with the idea ... f7-f5) 20 f4 ♛f5 21 ♞d6+! ♜xd6 22 cxd6 g6 23 ♜d5!!+-;

c) **19 ... ♝e7** 20 ♞xg7+ ♚f8 21 ♞h5 and Black is a pawn down without any compensation.

19	...	♞d4!

Karpov seizes the opportunity to centralize his knight and evict the white queen from her fine post on e2. Most importantly, he has won the psychological battle since Timman has failed to make the most out of his highly advantageous position.

20	♛g2	g6
21	♞hf6+	♚e7
22	♛f2?!	(69)

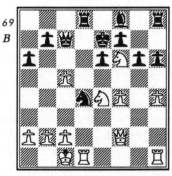

According to Timman, White

could still maintain some pressure by 22 ♘d6!?. The text move results in wholesale exchanges after the pseudo-combination which follows.

22	...	♕xf4+!
23	♕xf4	♘e2+
24	♔b1	♘xf4
25	♖xd8	♔xd8
26	♖d1+	♔c7
27	b4	♘d5
28	♘xd5+	exd5
29	♘f6	♔c6
30	♘xd5	g5

Black has managed to neutralize White's aggression and now proceeds to utilize his pawn majority on the kingside.

31 h5?!

Too optimistic. More to the point was the immediate **31 c4** trying to gain a tempo over the game continuation. After both **31 ... f5** 32 ♖e1 gxh4 33 ♖e5! and **31 ... gxh4** 32 ♖f1 a draw would be in sight.

31	...	f5
32	c4	f4
33	♖e1	f3
34	♖e6+	♔d7
35	♖f6	g4
36	♖f4	♗e7!

Black is already a little better.

37	♘xe7	♔xe7
38	♖xg4	♖f8
39	♖g1	♖f4
40	♖f1	♔e6 *(70)*

The picture has changed drastically. White has been forced to part with his strong knight and his rook occupies a

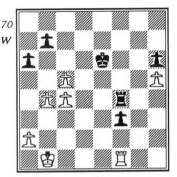

passive post in front of the dangerous f-pawn. Still, the position is a draw with correct defensive play.

41	♔c2	♖xc4+
42	♔d3	♖xb4
43	♖xf3	♖h4
44	♖f1	♖xh5
45	♖b1	♖xc5
46	♖xb7	♔d5
47	♖d7+?!	

Frustrated by the unexpected turn of events, Timman fails to spot his opponent's threat. If White wants to set up a defence along the fourth rank he should do it immediately by **47 ♖b6 ♖c6 48 ♖b4** when, in comparison with the game, Black cannot achieve the desired formation with pawns on a5 and h5 defended from the side by the black rook. Timman's suggestion of **47 ♖h7** should also be good enough for a draw.

47	...	♔e5
48	♖e7+?	

The last chance was **48 ♖h7**. Now Karpov achieves the position he was aiming for, and carries the day flawlessly with his inimitable technique.

48	...	♔f5
49	♖f7+	♔g6
50	♖f4	♔g5
51	♖a4	a5
52	♔e2	♖f5
53	♖a3	♔g4
54	♖c3	h5
55	♖c8	h4
56	♖g8+	♔g5

Also good is 56 ... ♔h3.

57	♖a8	♔g3
58	♔f1	♔f3
59	♖c8	♔e3
60	a4	♖g4
61	♖c5	*(71)*

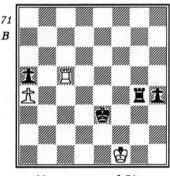

71
B

61	...	h3!

A terrible mistake would have been 61 ... ♖xa4?? 62 ♔g2! and the position is a theoretical draw, e.g. 62 ... ♖a1 63 ♖e5+ ♔d4 64 ♖f5! a4 65 ♖f4+ ♔e3 66 ♖f3+ ♔e4 67 ♖c3! ♔d4 68 ♖f3! and Black cannot make any progress. The only trap could be 68 ... a3 69 ♖b3 ♔c4 70 ♖f3 h3+ 71 ♖xh3?? ♔b4-+, but the calm 71 ♔h2! produces a drawn position.

62	♖e5+	

On 62 ♖c3+ Timman offers the following win: 62 ... ♔d2 63 ♖a3 (63 ♖xh3 ♖xa4 64 ♖h2+ ♔d1! 65 ♖h5 ♖f4+-+) 63 ... ♖e4!-+ (but not 63 ... ♔c2? 64 ♖xh3 ♖xa4 65 ♖h5 ♖f4+ 66 ♔e2 a4 67 ♖c5+ drawing).

62	...	♔f3
63	♖h5	♔g3
64	♔g1	♖xa4-+

The game is decided. White could have been spared the rest by resigning here, but was probably kicking himself for missing so many wins in the early phases of the struggle.

65 ♖g5+ ♔h4 66 ♖c5 ♖g4+ 67 ♔h2 a4 68 ♖c3 ♖g2+ 69 ♔h1 ♖g4 70 ♔h2 ♖g2+ 71 ♔h1 ♖g3 72 ♖c4+ ♖g4 73 ♖c3 ♖b4 74 ♖a3 ♖g4 75 ♖c3 ♔g5 76 ♔h2 ♖h4 0-1

An absorbing fight and a tribute to the art of defence!

Game 10
Timman – Seirawan
*Hilversum (2nd Match
Game) 1990*

1 e4 c6 2 d4 d5 3 e5 ♗f5 4 ♘c3 e6 5 g4 ♗g6 6 ♘ge2 c5 7 h4 h6 8 ♗e3

8	...	♕b6! *(72)*

Black's most flexible and aggressive continuation, this line is currently thought to give White quite a few headaches. Early queen outings always look suspicious, but this is hardly the case here: the queen gives ample protection to the

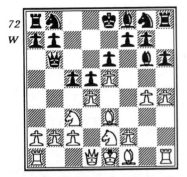

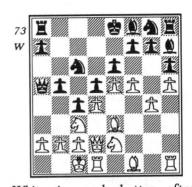

c-pawn while at the same time furthering Black's plans of attacking the centre and bringing the king to relative safety on the queenside.

9 f4!

Clearly the best. Dubious is **9 h5?!**, merely driving the bishop where it wants to go. Although it is also mentioned elsewhere, since even top players have committed this sin it is worth repeating that such an advance is only apparently aggressive and in reality loses time. Perhaps the most famous example is Nunn-Seirawan, Lugano 1983, which continued **9 ... ♗h7 10 ♕d2 ♘c6 11 0-0-0!? c4! 12 f4 ♕a5** (12 ... ♕a6!; 12 ... 0-0-0 is Game 8) **13 f5 b5** *(73)*
14 ♘xd5! b4! (not 14 ... ♕xa2 15 ♘dc3 ♕a1+ 16 ♘b1 ♘b4 17 ♘c3 or 17 ♕g2 with good play for White, while in the important variation 14 ... ♕xd2+ 15 ♗xd2 exd5 16 ♘c3 0-0-0 17 ♕g2 there is more than enough compensation for the piece, e.g. 17 ... ♘xd4 18 ♗e3 and now

White is much better after either 18 ... ♘c6 19 ♗xd5 ♘xe5 20 ♗b7+ or 18 ... b4 19 ♘xd5 ♘b5 {not 19 ... ♘c6 20 ♘b6+ axb6 21 ♗xc6 and Black's position is a mess} 20 ♗f1! etc.) **15 ♘c7+! ♕xc7 16 ♘f4 c3 17 ♕g2 ♘ge7 18 ♗c4** (wrong is 18 d5? exd5 19 ♘xd5 ♘xd5 20 ♖xd5 ♗e7∓, while 18 fxe6 b3! 19 exf7+ ♔d7 20 axb3 ♕a5 21 bxc3 ♕xc3 leads to an unclear position, according to Nunn) **18 ... 0-0-0 19 fxe6** (Nunn offers 19 d5! with an unclear position; however, my research shows that after 19 ... exd5 {not 19 ... ♕xe5 20 ♖he1 or 19 ... ♘xe5 20 ♗a6+ ♔b8 21 dxe6 with complications favouring White since the black army is split in two by the enemy pawn wedge and there are serious mate threats} 20 ♘xd5 ♘xd5 21 ♗xd5 Black should avoid both 21 ... ♕xe5 22 ♖he1 with great pressure, and 21 ... ♘xe5 22 ♗b7+ ♔b8 23 ♖xd8+ ♕xd8 24 ♗a6 when Black's faraway pieces lack the time to assist their king, e.g. 24 ... ♕c7 25 ♖d1 ♗e7 26 ♖d5 or 24

... ♕d7 25 ♖d1 cxb2+ 26 ♔xb2 ♘c4+ {or 26 ... ♗d6 27 ♖xd6 ♘c4+ 28 ♗xc4 ♕xd6 29 ♕e4 etc.} 27 ♗xc4 ♕xd1 28 ♗a6 with a winning attack for White; instead, he should play first the timely 21 ... cxb2+, since it is bad for White to play either 22 ♔b1 because in the last long variation the h1-rook cannot come to d1 as it will be captured with check or 22 ♔xb2 ♕xe5+ when the black queen gains time to take the undefended ♘e3) **19 ... ♔b8 20 exf7 cxb2+ 21 ♔b1 ♘a5!∓ 22 ♗d3 ♘c4 23 ♗xc4 ♕xc4 24 ♖h2 ♘d5 25 ♘xd5 ♖xd5!** (25 ... b3 26 axb3 ♕a6 27 ♔xb2 ♕a3+ 28 ♔c3 ♖xd5 29 ♔d2! is unclear according to Nunn) 26 e6?! b3 27 axb3 ♕a6 28 ♘f4+ ♔c8 29. ♔xb2 ♕a3+ 30 ♔c3 ♕a5+ 31 ♔b2 ♕a3+ 32 ♔c3 ♘b4+ 33 ♔c4 ♗e7 34 ♔c3 ♕a5+ 35 ♔b2 ♘a3+ 36 ♔b1 ♕c3 37 ♗c1 ♗xc1 38 ♔xc1 ♕a1+ 39 ♔d2 ♕xd4+ and 0-1. My analysis of Nunn's comments, along with the game Hendriks-Walker, European corr. Ch 1990, in which White attempted to improve one move earlier by playing **18 ♔b1 ♘ge7 19 ♗c4 0-0-0 20 d5 exd5 21 ♘xd5 ♘xd5 22 ♗xd5 ♘xe5 23 ♗b7+ ♔b8 24 ♖xd8+ ♕xd8 25 ♗a6 ♕d7 26 ♘f4 f6 27 ♖e1 b3 28 axb3 ♗a3 29 ♔a2 b1♕+ 30 ♔xb1 ♖e8 31 ♖e3 ♗g8 32 ♖d3 ♕c7 33 ♕e4 ♗e7 34 ♖c3 ♕d7 35 ♖d3 ♕c7** and ½-½, suggest that Black is at least equal in this line and the most White can hope for is a draw; therefore the whole idea may be dismissed as theoretically unsound.

Another option for White that has been tried at top level is **9 ♕d2**, encountered in A. Sokolov - Karpov, Linares Ct (9) 1987. They continued **9 ... ♘c6 10 0-0-0?!** *(74)*

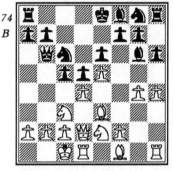

74
B

10 ... h5! 11 dxc5 ♗xc5 12 ♗xc5 ♕xc5 13 ♘f4 ♘ge7 14 ♘xg6 ♘xg6 15 f4 hxg4 16 h5 ♘ge7 17 ♗e2 ♕a5 18 a3 g3 19 ♗g4 b5 20 ♖hg1 b4 21 ♘b1 bxa3 22 ♘xa3 ♕xd2 23 ♖xd2 ♖b8 24 ♖xg3 g6 25 hxg6 ♘xg6 26 f5 ♖h1+ 27 ♖d1 ♖xd1+ 28 ♔xd1 exf5 29 ♗xf5 ♘ge7 30 ♗h3 ♘xe5 31 b3 ♖b4 32 ♘b1 f5 33 ♘c3 ♘f7 34 ♘e2 ♔f6 35 ♘c3 ♖h4 36 ♗g2 ♖h2 37 ♘f4 d4 38 ♖h3 ♖xh3 39 ♘xh3 ♘7g6 40 ♔d2 ♘h4 41 ♗b7 ♘hf3+ 42 ♔e2 d3+ 43 cxd3 ♘d4+ 44 ♔e3 ♘xb3 45 d4 ♘d7 46 ♗h1 ♘b6 47 ♔d3 ♘c1+ 48 ♔d2 ♘a2 49 ♘f4 ♘b4 50 ♔c3 a5 51 ♔b3 ♔e7 52 ♘g6+ ♔e6 53 ♘e5 ♘4d5 54 ♘c6 a4+ 55 ♔a3 ♘c7 56 ♔b4 ♔d6 57 ♘e5 ♘cd5+ 58 ♔a3 ♘e3 59 ♔b4 ♘c2+ 60

♗c3 ♘e3 61 ♔b4 ♔c7 62 ♘d3 ♘ec4 63 ♗g2 a3 64 ♔b3 ♘e3 65 ♗h1 ♘bc4 66 ♘e5 ♔d6 67 ♘xc4+ ♘xc4 68 ♗g2 f4 69 ♗h1 ♔e6 70 ♗g2 ♔f5 71 ♗h1 ♔g4 72 d5 ♔f5 73 d6 ♔e6 74 d7 ♔xd7 75 ♗d5 and ½–½.

It seems that Sokolov's idea is dubious, which makes it hard to understand the reason Karpov deviated from 8 ... ♕b6 in his ♗elfort game against Timman (9 f4! was not known at the time). Karpov later explained that 8 ... ♘c6?! was in fact a blunder, as he forgot the correct move order!

9 ... ♘c6

On **9 ... ♕xb2?** Nunn gives 10 f5 exf5 11 ♖b1 ♕a3 12 ♘xd5±. It is also worth noting that Black may not attempt to take advantage of the fact that the square f4 is now occupied in order to play **9 ... h5**, for similar reasons: after 10 f5 exf5 11 g5 the position is strategically lost.

10 f5 ♗h7!

Risky is 10 ... exf5 11 ♘f4! with a messy position, but favourable to White. Black voluntarily accepts that his bishop will be shut in, hoping to extricate it later under better circumstances.

11 ♕d2 0-0-0
12 0-0-0 c4

The strategy for both sides is clearly outlined: White would like to destroy the base of the black central pawn chain; Black

is playing for higher stakes since he is after the white king. A sharp game is the outcome, where the slightest mistake can lead to catastrophe, therefore this specific line is critical for the variation as a whole.

13 ♘f4 ♕a6!

Black is now poised for a massive attack on the queenside involving the pawn advance ... b7-b5-b4 as well as irritating invasions on b4 with the minor pieces. The best White can do is start grabbing pawns, both players burning the bridges behind them.

14 fxe6! b5

Naturally, the debate caused by this game continued in the years that followed. The encounter Prasad-Ravi, India 1991, saw Black winning quickly after **14 ... ♘b4** (! Seirawan) **15 exf7 ♘e7** (not 15 ... ♘xa2+? 16 ♘xa2 ♕xa2 17 ♕c3 ♘e7 18 ♕a3±, while the variation 17 ... ♗e4 18 fxg8♕ ♖xg8 19 ♖h3! a5 20 ♗g1! ♗b4 21 ♕a3!+- has already been mentioned in Chapter 1 under diagram 32) **16 a3 ♘xc2 17 g5?? ♘a1!** and 0-1. But of course, things are not that simple. Instead of 17 g5??, essential was **17 ♕f2** with an unclear position. White can also deviate earlier with **16 g5!?** when Thipsay offers the continuation **16 ... ♘xa2+ 17 ♘xa2 ♕xa2 18 ♕c3 ♗e4** as unclear. I disagree with this evaluation because of **19 ♕a3!**

♕xa3 20 ♘h3+ ♔b8 21 bxa3
♗xh1 22 ♖xh1 and White's
passed pawns are more than
enough compensation for the
exchange. A better try for
Black is **18 ... ♘c6!?**, as after
19 ♘xd5! ♖xd5 20 ♗xc4 ♕a4
(not 20 ... ♕a5 21 ♕xa5! ♖xa5 22
gxh6 gxh6 23 ♖hg1±) an exotic
position arises *(75)*:

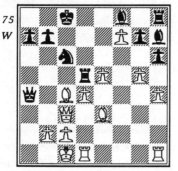

The threat ... ♘f8-b4 seems
devastating, but White can (and
must) sacrifice his queen by **21
♗xd5! ♗b4 22 ♗b3!** with
crazy complications:

1) **22 ... ♕a5** 23 gxh6! gxh6
(23 ... ♗xc3 24 bxc3 gxh6 25
♔b2) 24 ♕xc6+! bxc6 25 ♔b1
with the better chances for
White;

2) **22 ... ♕a1+** 23 ♔d2 ♕a5
(23 ... ♕xb2? 24 ♕xb4! ♘xb4 25
♖b1+-) 24 gxh6 gxh6 25 ♖hf1
when the position is difficult to
assess. My feeling is that the
pawn on f7 will gradually tie
all of Black's forces to its
blockade.

However, that is not the end
of the story. Instead of the
natural 19 ... ♖xd5, Black has

two interesting alternatives at
his disposal:

a) **19 ... ♗e4!?** (sacrificing a
third pawn, but it is evident
that the move creates dangerous threats) 20 ♗xc4 ♕a4 21 b3!
(21 ♘b3? ♕a6∓) 21 ... ♕a3+ (21 ...
♕a2 22 b4 ♕a4 23 ♕b3! ♕xb3 24
♗xb3 ♗xd5 25 ♗xd5 ♖xd5
seems better for White in view
of his mobile pawns) 22 ♔b1
♖xd5!? (22 ... ♗xd5 23 ♗c1 ♕e7
{23 ... ♕b4 24 ♕xb4 is ±} 24
♖hf1) with an unclear position.

b) **19 ... b5!?** (a cunning idea
from the Greek master Ioaki-
midis, but White is not without
resources) **20 ♔d2!** with a
wide choice for Black:

b1) **20 ... b4?** 21 ♕xc4 ♕xc4
22 ♗xc4 ♗e4 23 gxh6!±;

b2) **20 ... ♖xd5?!** 21 ♘h3+
♔b8 22 ♖a1 b4 (22 ... ♕xa1 23
♖xa1 ♗b4 24 ♗g2+-) 23 ♖xa2
bxc3+ 24 bxc3±;

b3) **20 ... ♗e4!?** 21 ♖a1!
(this has to be played immediately, as 21 ♘h3+? ♔b7 22 ♖a1
♗xh1! 23 ♖xa2 ♗xd5 is bad for
White in view of the unfortu-
nate position of the rook on a2
- compare with line b33 below)
and now:

b31) **21 ... ♗xh1** 22 ♖xa2
♗xd5 (threatening ... b5-b4 or
... ♘f8-b4) 23 ♖a6! b4 24 ♖xc6+
♔b7 25 ♕xc4+-;

b32) **21 ... b4** 22 ♘h3+ ♔b7
23 ♖xa2 bxc3+ 24 bxc3 ♗xd5 25
♖b1+±; after 24 ... ♗xh1? White,
despite being down a rook for
three pawns, exploits the in-

secure position of the black king by attacking directly: 25 ♖b2+ ♔a6 26 ♘c7+ ♔a5 (76)

27 d5! ♖xd5+ (27 ... ♗a3 28 ♖a2 ♔a4 29 ♘c5) 28 ♔e2! ♗a3 29 ♖a2 ♔a4 30 ♘xd5 ♗xd5 31 e6 and the threat 32 ♗c5 together with the passed pawns guarantee an easy win;

b33) **21 ... ♕xa1 22 ♘h3+ ♔b7 23 ♖xa1 ♗xd5 24 ♘f2! ♗b4 25 ♕xb4 ♘xb4 26 g6** when White's far advanced pawns may prove stronger than a rook;

b4) **20 ... ♔b8!?** (The idea of this move is to prevent White from transposing to the previous lines by ♗f1-h3 as that would be met by ... b5-b4, trapping the white queen) **21 b3!** (21 ♗e2?! is probably inadequate in view of 21 ... ♗e4! 22 ♖a1 ♗xh1! 23 ♖xa2 ♗xd5 24 e6! ♔b7! {worse is 24 ... b4? 25 ♗f4+ ♔b7 26 ♕e3 c3+ 27 bxc3 ♗xa2 28 ♕d3! with a strong attack, or 24 ... ♗b4?! 25 ♕xb4 ♘xb4 26 e7 ♘xa2 27 exd8♕+ ♖xd8 28 ♗f4+ ♔b7 29 g6} 25 ♗f4 {25 ♔c1 ♗b4 26 e7 ♗xc3 27 exd8♘+ ♘xd8 28 bxc3 hxg5∓} 25 ... ♗b4 26 ♕xb4 ♘xb4 27 e7 ♗xf7! 28 exd8♕ ♖xd8 and White is in trouble as his pawn on d4 is hanging) **21 ... ♖xd5 22 ♖a1 b4! 23 ♖xa2 bxc3+ 24 ♔xc3** reaching a complex endgame (77):

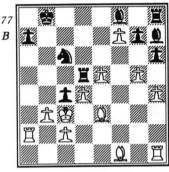

White has three pawns for a piece and, at first glance, his king seems exposed. However, closer inspection shows that it is by no means easy to take advantage of this factor:

b41) **24 ... ♗b4+ 25 ♔xc4 ♗e4** suggests itself. If White mechanically reacts by **26 gxh6?** a horrible surprise is in store for him: 26 ... a5!! (Threatening 27 ... ♘xe5+ and 28 ... ♖c8#!) 27 ♘h3 ♗xh1!! 28 hxg7 ♘xe5+! 29 dxe5 ♖xh4+ mating anyway.

However, there is a way out in **26 ♖a6!**. Despite the huge material investments this move entails it has the advantage of breaking the mating nets and sufficiently disturbing the coordination of the black pieces. After **26 ... ♗xh1 27 ♖xc6**

White gets four pawns and tremendous activity for the sacrificed rook but the real point of 26 ♖a6! is revealed only after **26 ... ♔b7** 27 ♖xc6! ♔xc6 28 ♗xb4 ♖b8+ 29 ♔a3 ♗xh1 30 gxh6 gxh6 31 c4! when White's four connected passed pawns look like a tidal wave capable of overcoming all kinds of resistance. A truly remarkable case!;

b42) **24 ... cxb3** 25 cxb3 ♗e4 is met by 26 ♗g2. If Black plays 25 ... ♗b4+ first, then after 26 ♔b2 ♗e4 (26 ... ♘xd4 27 ♗c4±) White has the intermediate move 27 gxh6 to be followed by ♖h1-g1. Also worth analysing after 25 ... ♗b4+ is the daring 26 ♔c4!?;

b43) Finally, the intriguing **24 ... ♗e4!?** might well be Black's best. After 25 bxc4 ♖xd4 (25 ... ♗b4+ 26 ♔b3 is also unclear) 26 ♖b2+ ♔c7 27 ♖g1 an unclear position is reached with many tactical chances for both sides.

Let us return to the main game, after Seirawan's bold 14 ... b5:

    15   exf7   ♘ge7
    16   ♘e6   b4 *(78)*

The fight has warmed up unusually rapidly as a result of Black's double pawn sacrifice for the initiative. Black's forces on the queenside are extremely menacing, so it seems the wrong moment for material-istic thoughts; White must give

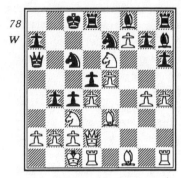

up a piece in order to stay alive.

    17   ♘xd8?

An indication that White has not evaluated the situation properly, as now Black obtains an overwhelming attack. Tim-man should have preserved his agile knight by **17 ♘c5!**, reaching an unclear position: after **17 ... bxc3** (Seirawan points out 17 ... ♕a5 18 ♘3a4 ♗b8 19 ♖b1 ♘c8 20 b3 ♘b6 21 e6 ♗xc5 22 ♘xc5 c3 23 ♕h2+!) **18 ♕xc3 ♕xa2** (18 ... ♕a5!?) **19 ♗h3±** (analysis by Timman) White has two pawns plus positional pressure for the piece, but Black's chances should not be underestimated.

    17   ...   ♔xd8!
    18   a3! *(79)*

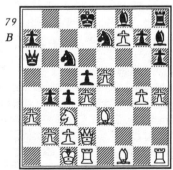

The only move to avoid immediate disaster.

18 ... bxc3?

Failing to reap the fruits of his labour. As Seirawan himself points out in *Inside Chess*, 18 ... bxa3! would have been deadly. I quote the American Grandmaster's analysis:

a) 19 ♘a2 axb2+ 20 ♔xb2 (20 ♔b1 ♘c8 with the idea ... ♘c6-b4 wins) 20 ... ♘c8 21 c3 ♕b5+ 22 ♔a1 ♘a5 23 ♘c1 ♕b1#;

b) 19 ♔b1 ♘b4 20 ♖c1 ♘ec6 21 b3 and now 21 ... ♘xc2-+ or 21 ... ♘a5-+;

c) 19 ♕g2!? ♕a5!-+.

19 ♕xc3 ♘c8
20 g5!

The pawn on f7 needs support from an open g-file to prove its strength. As it soon becomes evident, Black's mistake on the 18th move has granted White excellent fighting chances.

20 ... ♘b6
21 gxh6 gxh6
22 ♗d2!

Overprotecting the critical b4 square and giving his queen freedom of movement along the third rank, White intends to meet the apparently crushing 22 ... ♘b4? by 23 ♕xb4! ♗xb4 24 ♗xb4 (Seirawan), when Black is completely lost despite his material advantage.

22 ... ♕a4!
23 ♔b1 a5
24 ♖g1 ♗b4
25 ♖g8+?

Timman's intention undoubtedly was to divert the black bishop from its deadly surveillance of c2. However, an excellent piece of analysis by John van der Wiel proves that White missed a winning continuation here. I quote the Dutch GM's analysis from the magazine *Inside Chess*:

"25 ♖g8+ is in fact a mistake. Timman should have played **25 axb4!**, when Black has two recaptures:

a) **25 ... ♘xb4** 26 ♖g8+ ♔c7 (26 ... ♔d7 27 e6+ is no improvement, while 26 ... ♖xg8 27 fxg8♕+ ♗xg8 28 b3 ♕a2+ 29 ♔c1 cxb3 30 cxb3 ♗h7 31 ♕b2 wins for White) 27 b3!!:

a1) **27 ... ♕xb3+** 28 ♕xb3 cxb3; White now has his choice of 29 f8♕ or 29 ♗xb4 bxc2+ 30 ♔c1 cxd1♕+ 31 ♔xd1 ♖xg8 32 fxg8♕+ ♗xg8 33 ♗xa5 winning;

a2) **27 ... ♕a2+** 28 ♔c1 ♗xc2 29 ♕b2 stops Black's attack;

b) **25 ... axb4** (the recapture intended by Seirawan) **26 ♖g8+!** ♔c7! (26 ... ♖xg8 27 fxg8♕+ ♗xg8 28 ♕f3 causes an unpleasant interruption of Black's attack. If 28 ... b3 {28 ... ♕xc2+ gives White the better ending} 29 ♕f8+! ♔c7 30 ♕g7+ ♘d7 31 cxb3 cxb3 32 ♗c3 is good for White. The series of queen checks is to dominate the black bishop) **27 f8♕** (this is best; if 27 ♖xh8 then 27 ... b3!! is a rude awakening) **27 ... bxc3 28 ♖g7+ ♘d7 29 ♕d6+ ♔b6 30**

♖xh7 ♖xh7 **31 ♗xc3** and with his extra pawns White should win."

25 ... ♖xg8!

On 25 ... ♗xg8? Timman's recommendation of 26 axb4 ♗xf7 27 bxa5 seems better for White. In mutual time-trouble, Black rightly prefers to keep his dangerous bishop.

26 fxg8♕+ ♗xg8
27 ♕f3! ♘xd4!
28 ♕f6+ ♔c7
29 ♕g6 *(80)*

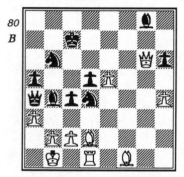

29 ... ♗c5??

van der Wiel discovered **29 ... ♗e6!** ("probably missed under the influence of time trouble and the sudden domination of the g8-bishop - a psychological block, also working during the post-mortem"), when White is defenceless. "Even after the best line 30 ♘f4 (30 ♗xb4 ♗f5 31 ♘d6+ ♔b7 32 ♕h5 ♖xc2+ 33 ♔a1 ♘a4) 30 ... ♗f5 31 e6+ ♔b7! 32 ♕g7+ ♔c6! 33 ♕xd4 ♕xc2+ 34 ♔a1 (very attractive is 34 ♔a2 c3 35 ♗c1 ♕b1+ 36 ♔b3 ♗c2#) 34 ... c3 White has to give up."

30 ♗e3 ♘xc2
31 ♗xc5 ♘xa3+
32 ♔c1 ♘d7
33 ♗xa3 c3
34 ♕d6+ ♔d8

Black's flag fell in this hopeless position.

It is quite notable that Timman, in his notes to this game (published in *Informator 50*), gives 25 ♖g8! as the only move and fails to spot 29 ... ♗e6!, thinking that White wins after 29 ♕g6. I can explain this slip through my personal experience, knowing that chessplayers are asked to comment on important games during tournaments or immediately after, when the nervous tension is still there.

1-0

This is probably the most important game for the assessment of the 4 ♘c3 e6 variation.

Game 11
Kotronias – Speelman
New York 1990

1 e4 c6 2 d4 d5 3 e5 ♗f5 4 ♘c3 e6 5 g4 ♗g6 6 ♘ge2 c5 7 h4 h6 8 ♗e3

8 ... cxd4
9 ♘xd4 ♗b4 *(81)*

In this continuation Black plays simple chess, trying to complete the development of his pieces as quickly as possible without worrying about small concessions in the centre. This is an acceptable method, since the bishop move prepares a comfortable development of the king's knight.

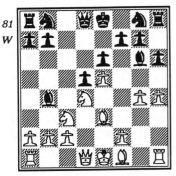

81
W

10 h5 ♗h7!

The best move in the position. **10 ... ♗e4** (given an ! by Seirawan) was played in Timman-Seirawan, Tilburg 1990, but it seems to me that inserting f2-f3 favours White. After **11 f3 ♗h7** the game continued **12 ♗d3 ♗xd3 13 ♕xd3 ♘d7 14 0-0-0 ♗xc3! 15 ♕xc3 ♖c8 16 ♕e1 ♘xe5 17 ♗f4 ♘c6 18 ♘f5 ♔f8! 19 ♗d6+ ♘ge7 20 ♘xe7 ♘xe7 21 ♕e5! ♔g8! 22 ♗xe7 ♕xe7 23 ♖xd5 ♕c7 24 ♕xc7 ♖xc7 25 ♖b5?** (Seirawan suggests 25 ♖d8+ with a slight advantage for White, while now it is Black who gets the upper hand) **25 ... ♔f8 26 f4 ♔e7 27 b3 ♖d8 28 ♖d1 ♖xd1+ 29 ♔xd1 ♔d6 30 a4 a6 31 ♖b4 e5 32 ♔d2 exf4 33 ♖xf4 ♔e5 34 ♖f5+ ♔e6 35 c4 g6 36 ♖d5 f5 37 gxf5+ gxf5 38 ♔e3 ♖g7 39 ♔d4 ♖g3 40 ♖e5+ ♔f6 41 b4 ♖a3 42 a5 ♖a4 43 ♔d5 ♖xb4 44 ♖e6+ ♔g5 45 ♖b6 ♖a4 46 ♖xb7 ♖xa5+ 47 c5 ♔xh5 48**

♖b1 f4 49 ♔d6 ♖a2 50 ♖c1 ♖d2+ 51 ♔e6 ♔g4 52 c6 ♖d8 53 c7 ♖c8 54 ♔d7 ♖xc7+ 55 ♖xc7 f3 56 ♔d6 f2 57 ♖g7+ ♔f3 58 ♖f7+ ♔e2 59 ♖e7+ ♔d2 60 ♖f7 ♔e1 61 ♖e7+ ♔f1 62 ♖h7 a5 63 ♔c5 ♔e2 and ½–½.

However, the natural **12 ♕d2!** is stronger, for example 12 ... ♘d7 13 a3! ♗xc3?! (13 ... ♗a5 is better, but 14 f4! ♘e7 {... ♘d7-c5 is no longer possible} 15 ♗d3 leaves White on top) 14 ♕xc3 ♘xe5 15 ♗b5+ ♘d7 16 ♘f5! exf5 17 0-0-0! with a tremendous attack on Black's exposed king (82):

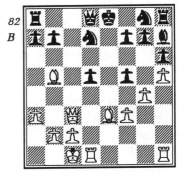

82
B

The point is that with the pawn on f3 there is no defence by interposing the knight on e4 after 17 ... ♘f6 18 ♗c5 ♕c7 19 ♖he1+. Thus, relatively best for Black is to decline the sacrifice by playing 16 ... ♗xf5 17 gxf5 ♘f6, although the bishop pair and the open g-file give White good chances for a successful onslaught.

11 ♕d2

Another important option here is **11 ♗d3 ♗xd3 12 ♕xd3**

♘d7 13 ♗d2!? *(83)* (13 0-0-0 is similar to Timman-Seirawan mentioned above, while 13 f4 ♖c8 14 ♗d2 ♗xc3!? 15 ♗xc3 ♘c5 is difficult to evaluate as Black gets e4 for his knight)

13 ... ♖c8 (13 ... ♗xc3 14 ♕xc3 ♖c8 15 ♕e3) **14 0-0-0!?**, with a complicated struggle ahead, slightly favourable to the first player.

11 ...   ♘d7
12 a3?!   ♗a5?!

Black should have grabbed the e-pawn by 12 ... ♗xc3! 13 ♕xc3 ♘xe5 as there is no clear refutation at White's disposal.

13 b4?

White thoughtlessly over-extends on the queenside. Correct was 13 f4! keeping a slight advantage, while now the balance swings slightly towards Black's side.

13 ...   ♗b6!
14 f4

Seirawan gives '14 f4±'. In the *post-mortem* Speelman and I agreed that the position is unclear, but when I analysed alone I could not find a proper

place for my king and conluded that the position is unsatisfactory for White.

14 ...   ♘e7
15 ♘cb5?

Appropriate here is 15 ♗d3, but White persists in an attacking approach while his king is still unsafe.

15 ...   0-0
16 ♘d6?   ♘c6!

Now Black is almost winning, since White suffers from much worse development. The d6-knight, being isolated from fellow pieces may prove to be a liability instead of the hoped-for powerhouse.

17 ♘xc6   bxc6
18 ♗d3 *(84)*

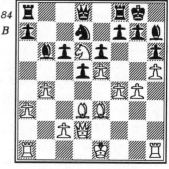

18 ...   f6!

Undermining the foundation of White's outpost.

19 ♗xh7+   ♔xh7
20 ♗xb6   axb6
21 ♕d3+   ♔g8
22 0-0-0   c5?

Trying to be "fancy" where simple means are effective. Speelman saw during the game the correct **22 ... fxe5** 23 g5 exf4! 24 ♕g6 (24 gxh6? ♘e5) 24 ... ♕e7 25 gxh6 ♖f6! 26 ♕g5 ♔h7, but was afraid of 27 ♘e4 which achieves nothing after 27 ... dxe4 28 hxg7 ♕xg7 29 ♖xd7 ♖f7 30 ♖xf7 ♕xf7 and White is clearly lost.

| 23 | ♕g6! | ♕e7 |
| 24 | g5 | |

Due to Black's 22nd move mistake, White has taken over the initiative. This opening is difficult to handle indeed!

24	...	fxg5
25	f5!	♘xe5
26	♕xe6+	♕xe6
27	fxe6	♖f6
28	♘b5!	♖c8
29	e7!	♖e6 *(85)*

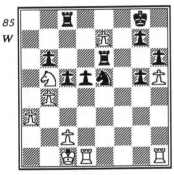

85
W

30 e8♕+!

A rare but noteworthy motif. No matter how Black recaptures, he must surrender the exchange.

| 30 | ... | ♖cxe8 |
| 31 | ♘c7 | |

As a result of all the complications, White even enjoys a slight advantage here. Nevertheless, Speelman manages to find enough counterplay to nullify any danger.

31	...	cxb4
32	axb4	♘f3!
33	♘xe8	♖xe8
34	♖xd5	g4

This advance guarantees Black adequate counterchances. Having survived a near disaster, I decided to settle for a draw, ignoring the fact I was an exchange up.

35	♖f1	♖e2
36	♖f5?!	g6!
37	hxg6?!	♔g7
38	♖5xf3	

The ending is drawn, as both sides will sacrifice their rook for the enemy passed pawn, therefore ...

½-½

This is the only time I have ever been in danger while playing the Caro Advance Variation, while it is obvious that improvements for White are available. Since I have essayed 3 e5 against many strong grandmasters (Speelman was at his peak when this game was played), I believe this fact is enough in itself to demonstrate the inherent strength of the 4 ♘c3 system.

Conclusion

6 ... c5 is hard to crack, but it leads to the sort of game that 3 e5 players usually aim for: sharp positions, full of thrust and counterthrust, demanding excellent preparation and understanding of the dynamic

aspects of the opening. Many lines are quite entertaining, but when you are sitting at the board you do not always think the same!

Summing up, it seems that the future of the Caro Advance Variation as a whole will be mostly determined by developments in this line.

3 The 4 ... ♛b6 Variation

Game 12
Nimzowitsch – Capablanca
New York 1927

The game that follows was awarded a special prize for the best played game in the tournament. After a dubious opening, Capablanca manages to freeze his opponent's demonstration on the kingside and wins elegantly by penetrating the enemy position with his heavy pieces. The ideas behind the opening of this game have been analysed in some detail in Chapter 1, therefore here the analysis will concentrate more on the middlegame aspects.

1 e4 c6 2 d4 d5 3 e5 ♗f5
4   ♗d3?!

I quote Irving Chernev's annotation from his book *Capablanca's Best Chess Endings* (Atkins-Capablanca, London 1922): "White hastens to get rid of his good bishop, a strategic error repeated by Nimzowitsch in his famous 1927 encounter against Capablanca". Wise words, but for the wrong reason! The truth is that Chernev's comment is absolutely

correct, since it accompanies White's 4th and not his 5th move (in the above-mentioned games White unwisely exchanged his good bishop before Black moved his queen to b6). However, this is merely a result of hero-worship rather than objective thinking, as Capablanca continued in both games with a direct transposition to our analysis, and was still praised by Chernev.

4   ...   ♗xd3
5   ♕xd3   e6
6   ♘c3   ♕b6?!
7   ♘ge2   c5?!

A premature thrust. More to the point is 7 ... ♘e7, as we shall see in the next three games. Another option is 7 ... ♕a6, but it will be analysed in Kotronias-Khalifman (Game 14) since after 7 ... ♘e7 8 0-0 ♕a6 it transposes.

8   dxc5   ♗xc5
9   0-0   ♘e7?!

9 ... ♘d7 10 ♘a4 ♕c7 11 ♘xc5 ♕xc5 12 ♕g3 ♘e7 13 ♕xg7 ♖f8 14 ♕xh7 ♘xe5 15 ♗e3 ♕c7 16 ♘d4 ♘5g6 17 ♕h3 a6 18 ♖fe1 0-0-0 19 ♗g5± Kotronias-Gausel, Reykjavik 1988; White's

plan is to follow up with ♛h3-g3, h2-h4.

10 ♞a4?!

The opening play has been inaccurate, but in those days people tended to focus their attention more on the middle-game. To set the historical record straight, White misses a good chance to gain the advantage by **10 b4!** *(86)*

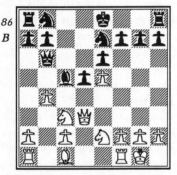

86
B

This was missed not only by Nimzowitsch, but also by various commentators (including Chernev). After 10 ... ♛xb4 (10 ... ♝xb4 11 ♜b1 ♛a5 12 ♞b5±) 11 ♞b5 ♞a6 12 ♝a3 ♛a5 13 ♝xc5 ♞xc5 14 ♞d6+ ♚d7 15 ♛g3 ♜hg8 16 ♞xf7 White gets a clear advantage. The game continuation is much less enterprising, playing into Capa's hands.

10	...	♛c6
11	♞xc5	♛xc5
12	♝e3	♛c7
13	f4	♞f5
14	c3?!	

Preferable was Alekhine's recommendation of **14 ♝f2** (to be followed by c2-c4), when

White might still have counted on an advantage. One gets the impression that Nimzowitsch's play is a little too passive for the occasion.

14	...	♞c6
15	♜ad1	g6
16	g4??	

And now he bursts forth with this inopportune gesture. In fact this is a positional blunder, allowing Capa to stabilize the pawn structure on the kingside.

16	...	♞xe3
17	♛xe3	*(87)*

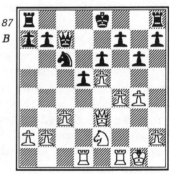

87
B

| 17 | ... | h5! |

Analysts have failed to comment on this, considering White's reply forced. However, as the next note proves, the move demanded precise calculations and deep evaluation of a certain position.

18 g5?!

Losing kingside pawn mobility, but others were uninspiring:

a) **18 h3?** hxg4 19 hxg4 0-0-0-+ as Black threatens both ... ♜h8-h4 and ... g6-g5;

b) **18 f5 gxf5** (18 ... ♛xe5? 19

♛xe5 ♘xe5 20 fxe6 fxe6 21 ♘d4 is equal) **19 gxf5 0-0-0!** (19 ... ♘xe5? 20 fxe6 fxe6 21 ♘d4 0-0-0 22 ♘b5±) and now:

b1) **20 ♘f4** ♘xe5! 21 fxe6 fxe6 22 ♖de1!? (22 ♘xe6 ♘g4! 24 ♛d2 ♛b6+ 25 ♘d4 ♛g6!∓; 22 ♛xa7 ♖hg8+ 23 ♔h1 ♛c6∓) 22 ... ♘g4! 23 ♛a7 (on 23 ... ♛xe6+ ♔b8, threatening ... ♖hf8) 23 ... ♖hg8 24 ♔h1 ♖df8 25 ♛a4 (after 25 ♛a8+ ♔d7 26 ♛a4+ ♛c6 27 ♛xc6+ bxc6 28 h3 ♘h6 29 ♘xh5 ♘f5 Black has more than enough compensation for the pawn because of his active king and central pawn roller) 25 ... ♛d6! (preparing ... e6-e5, or ... ♔c8-b8) with excellent chances for Black; 26 ♖xe6? is a bad mistake because of 26 ... ♖xf4! 27 ♛a8+ ♔c7 28 ♛a5+ ♔b8 29 ♖xd6 ♖xf1+ 30 ♔g2 ♘e3++ with mate soon to follow.

b2) **20 ♘d4** (relatively best) 20 ... ♛b6! 21 ♔h1 (21 ♛h3 ♔b8! 22 ♔h1 ♘xd4 23 cxd4 ♖c8∓) 21 ... ♖hg8 22 ♛h3 ♘xd4 23 cxd4 ♔b8! and Black is better because he has a safer king.

18   ...   0-0

Black has a strategically won game. His king is safe on the kingside while on the other wing he enjoys the prospect of a minority attack. However, the way in which Capablanca makes use of his advantages is a priceless lesson for every chessplayer.

19   ♘d4   ♛b6

20	♖f2	♖fc8
21	a3	♖c7
22	♖d3	♘a5
23	♖e2	♖e8
24	♔g2	♘c6
25	♖ed2	♖ec8
26	♖e2	♘e7!
27	♖ed2	♖c4

Capa's plans begin to take shape. His knight is ready to jump to f5 in order to challenge White's stronghold on d4. That would allow his rooks to penetrate into the heart of the enemy position.

28	♛h3?!	♔g7
29	♖f2	a5
30	♖e2	♘f5!
31	♘xf5+	gxf5
32	♛f3	

On 32 ♛xh5? the reply 32 ... ♖h8 33 ♛f3 ♖h4 wins easily.

32   ...   ♔g6 *(88)*

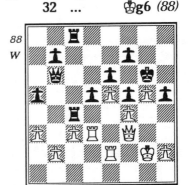

Everything goes as planned. In the next few moves Black improves the positions of his pieces, by slowly infiltrating through the half-open c-file.

33	♖ed2	♖e4
34	♖d4	♖c4
35	♛f2	♛b5

36 ♔g3   ♖cxd4!

Abandoning the plan of a minority attack by ... ♛b5–b3, ... b7–b5–b4, as he gets the chance to create a new weakness on d4. White cannot recapture with the rook in view of the reply 37 ... ♖e2, winning instantly.

37 cxd4   ♛c4
38 ♔g2   b5!
39 ♔g1   b4
40 axb4   axb4
41 ♔g2   ♛c1!

Capablanca is tightening the noose move by move. No doubt, Nimzowitsch must have felt extremely uncomfortable during the final phase of the game.

42 ♔g3   ♛h1!
43 ♖d3

The only move. On 43 ♖e2 (trying to prevent ... ♖e4–e1), the simplest is 43 ... ♖xe2 44 ♛xe2 ♛g1+, winning the d-pawn.

43 ...   ♖e1
44 ♖f3   ♖d1
45 b3

White has entered a zugzwang situation. The proof:

a) **45 h3 ♖g1+ 46 ♔h4 ♖g4#!**;
b) **45 ♔h3 ♖d2!–+**;
c) **45 ♖e3 ♖f1 46 ♛e2 ♛g1+–+**;
d) **45 ♖b3 ♛e4–+**.

45 ...   ♖c1!
46 ♖e3   ♖f1 (89)
0–1

A masterly conclusion by a great champion.

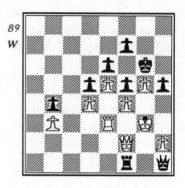

89
W

Game 13
Kotronias – King
New York 1990

1 e4 c6 2 d4 d5 3 e5 ♗f5 4 ♘c3

4   ...   ♛b6 (90)

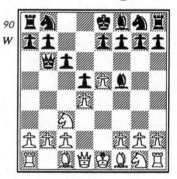

90
W

This is the main alternative to 4 ... e6. Black wants to avoid the labyrinth of variations already examined and steer the game to positional channels. For quite some time 4 ... ♛b6 was successful as most players with White concentrated their efforts on the risky continuation **5 g4!? ♗d7**. However, it seems extravagant to play 5 g4 when the black bishop still has the option to retreat to d7; the resulting positions closely resemble the French except for the extra move g2-g4, which looks more like a weakness than a threatening gesture. For example, White's overextension gave him no advantage in the game Timman-Kamsky, Tilburg 1990, after 6 ♞a4 ♛c7 7 ♗e3 (*Editor's note:* 7 ♞c5 e6 8 ♞d3 h5∓ Klinger-Hodgson, Oakham 1984) 7 ... e6 8 ♗g2 ♞e7 9 f4 ♞a6!? 10 ♞f3 h5 11 h3 ♞g6 12 ♞c3 ♗e7 13 ♛e2 ♞h4 14 ♞xh4 ♗xh4+ **15 ♗f2 ♗xf2+** 16 ♛xf2 hxg4 17 hxg4 0-0-0 18 0-0-0 c5!. Kamsky suggests 15 ♔f1 ♗e7 16 gxh5 0-0-0 17 ♗f3 as a possible improvement for White, but I do not know many players who would be willing to venture this.

5 ♗d3!?

White exchanges his 'good' bishop for the sake of quick development. Although this may not suit everyone's style, practice has shown that it is not easy for Black to reach equality. Remarkably enough, Seirawan's recent book on the Caro Advance does not even mention this move at this specific moment; our Main Game and others are mentioned there only through transpositions, even though the correct move order is 4 ♞c3 and only after 4 ... ♛b6, 5 ♗d3.

5 ... ♗xd3

Extremely risky is **5 ...**

♛xd4?!. After **6 ♞f3!? ♛g4 7 h3:**

a) **7 ... ♛xg2** 8 ♖g1 ♛xh3 9 ♗f1 ♗xc2 (9 ... ♛h5 10 ♖g5 ♗xc2 11 ♛xc2 ♛xf3 12 ♗g2+-) 10 ♛e2 (10 ♛xc2!?), e.g. **10 ... ♛h5?** 11 ♖g5 ♛h1 12 ♛xc2 ♛xf3 13 ♗g2; therefore Black must retreat with **10 ... ♛c8** and face a strong attack in exchange for a minimal material investment by White. *Editor's note:* Lassen-Bergmann, Danish League 1991/92 saw Black try **10 ... ♛d7** but then he had problems developing: 11 ♛xc2 e6 12 ♗e3 ♞e7 13 ♞d4 ♞f5 14 ♞xf5 exf5 15 0-0-0 g6 16 ♗c4 ♛c7 (16 ... ♗g7 17 ♞xd5 cxd5 18 ♞xd5 0-0 19 ♞f6+ ♗xf6 20 ♖xd7 ♞xd7 21 ♛xf5) 17 ♖xd5! ♞d7 18 ♖xd7 ♛xd7 19 ♖d1 ♛xd1+ 20 ♛xd1 ♗g7 21 ♗xf7+ 1-0.

b) **7 ... ♛h5** 8 0-0 ♗xd3 9 cxd3 e6 10 ♛b3 (Lars Bo Hansen suggests 10 ♞e2 - ed.) White has a huge lead in development and some ideas to embarrass the black queen by ♞c3-e2-f4.

Editor's note: instead of 9 ... e6 in this line, **9 ... ♛f5** was tried in the game Borge-K. Berg, Espergærde 1992: 10 ♖e1 ♛c8 11 e6 fxe6 12 ♞d4 ♞a6 13 ♛f3! ♞f6 14 g4 h6 15 ♗f4 g5 16 ♗d6! ♔f7 17 ♖xe6 ♛xe6 (17 ... c5 fails to, e.g. 18 ♖ae1 cxd4 19 ♗xe7 ♗xe7 20 ♖xe7+ ♔g6 21 ♞xd5 ♖f8 22 ♞xf6 ♖xf6 23 ♛e4+ {Borge} or 18 ♞xd5 cxd4 19 ♖xf6+! {L. Hansen} 18 ♞xe6

exd6?! (18 ... ♚xe6 19 ♗h2 ♚f7
20 ♖e1 ♗g7 21 ♛e3 e5!? 22 ♘xe5
♖he8 is a better try according
to L. Hansen) 19 ♖e1 ♘c5 20
♛f5 ♖e8 21 ♘xg5+! hxg5 22
♖xe8 ♚xe8 23 ♛xf6 ♖xh3 24
♛g6+ ♚d7 25 ♛xg5 ♖xd3 26
♛f5+ ♚e7 27 ♛h7+ ♚d8 28 ♛f7
(with its superior back-up, the
white g-pawn proves much
faster than its black counterpart on the d-file) 28 ... ♘d7 29
g5 ♖d4 30 f3 ♖h4 31 ♘e2! d4 32
♘f4 ♖xf4 33 ♛xf4 ♗g7 34 ♛f7
♗h8 35 ♛g8+ 1-0.

Also interesting is Patrick
Wolff's suggestion of **6 ♘ce2!**,
with the following possibilities:

a) **6 ... ♛xe5?!** 7 ♘f3 ♛f6 8
♗g5 ♛e6 9 ♘d4 ♛g6 10 ♗xf5
♛xg5 11 ♗c8! with the better
position for White e g 11 ... a6 12
♗xb7 ♖a7 13 ♗xc6+ ♘xc6 14
♘xc6 ♖c7 15 c4! and the black
king is exposed.

b) **6 ... ♛g4!?** 7 f3! ♛xg2 8
♗xf5 ♛xh1 when the black
queen seems to be in danger
but there is no clear way to
capture it.

6   ♛xd3   e6

Forced. On 6 ... ♛a6?, 7 e6!
♛xd3 8 exf7+ ♚xf7 9 cxd3 e6 10
f4 is ±, Ufimtsev-Ravkin, USSR
1961.

7   ♘ge2

And there we have it! After
no less than 63 years the opening of Nimzowitch-Capablanca
is repeated in the same city.
Could this be Christened the
"New York Variation"?

7   ...   ♘d7

This time Black chooses a
solid continuation. Also possible are 7 ... ♘e7 and 7 ... ♛a6.

8   0-0   ♘e7 (*91*)

Transposing again to 7 ...
♘e7 8 0-0 ♘d7.

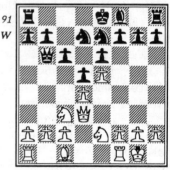

9   a4   c5

The alternatives 9 ... a6 and 9
... a5 are examined in Game 15,
Kotronias-Tukmakov.

10   a5   ♛c6?!

Black's queen is exposed on
this square. Preferable was 10
... ♛d8! 11 ♗g5!? with a complex struggle ahead.

11   dxc5   ♘xe5?

After **11 ... ♘xc5!** 12 ♛f3!
(Speelman) White has only a
slight edge. The text is wrong
on the basis that one should
not open up the centre when
lagging in development.

12   ♛g3   ♘5g6 (*92*)

Playing the other knight to
g6 would encourage an advance
of White's f-pawn, but now the
f8-bishop will remain blocked
long enough for White to build
up a strong initiative.

13   ♘d4!   ♛xc5

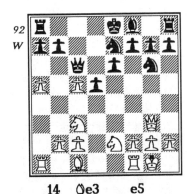

14   ♗e3   e5

Forced, since on any queen retreat, 15 ♘cb5 is crushing.

15   ♘db5   ♕c6 *(93)*

On 15 ... d4? I intended 16 ♗xd4! exd4 17 ♘c7+ ♚d8 18 ♘xa8 dxc3 19 ♖fd1+ ♚c8 20 ♘b6+! mating quickly.

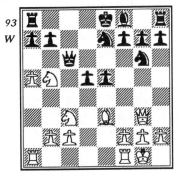

16   a6!

The most difficult move of the game. White had to resist the temptation of recovering his pawn by 16 ♘xa7?! as that would be equivalent to surrendering the initiative. The text, on the other hand, has the dual advantage of 'installing' a knight on b5 as well as creating a useful asset in the shape of the dangerous a-pawn. From a strategic point of view, the game has already been decided.

16   ...   b6

16 ... bxa6? 17 ♖xa6! is the tactical justification of the previous move.

17   ♖ad1!   d4
18   ♕h3!?

18 ♘e4! ♘d5 19 c4!± is more exact, but I was obsessed with the idea of sacrificing something on d4 (18 ♗xd4? ♘f5∓).

18   ...   ♘c8 *(94)*

Black can hardly capture either piece as, in that case, the check on d6 would be murderous:

a) **18 ... dxe3?** 19 ♘d6+ ♚d8 20 ♘cb5!+−;

b) **18 ... dxc3?** 19 ♘d6+ ♚d8 20 ♘xf7+ and now:

b1) **20 ... ♚c7** 21 ♖d6 ♕xd6 (21 ... ♕e8 22 ♖fd1+−) 22 ♘xd6 ♚xd6 23 ♖d1++−;

b2) **20 ... ♚e8** 21 ♘d6+ ♚d8 22 b4! ♘d5 (22 ... ♚c7 23 b5 ♕d7 24 ♕f3 ♖b8 25 ♖d3!+−) 23 ♕f3! ♗xd6 (23 ... ♘xb4 24 ♕f7!! ♗xd6 25 ♗g5+ ♚c8 26 ♖xd6!+−) 24 ♖xd5 ♚c7 (24 ... ♚e7 25 ♗g5+ ♚e6? {25 ... ♚e8 26 ♖xd6±} 26 ♕g4+! ♚xd5 27 ♖d1♯) 25 b5 ♕c4 26 ♖c5+!+−.

Of course, I did not have to calculate all the above lines in detail. The pawn on a6 is a bone in Black's throat, creating dangerous mating threats.

19   ♗xd4!   ♘d6

Trying to get rid of the annoying knight. **19 ... exd4** is simply out of the question,

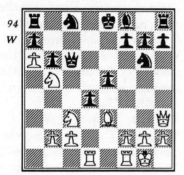

94
W

while on **19 ... ♗d6** White responds with 20 ♘e3 0-0 21 ♕f3!, entering a winning endgame.

20 ♖fe1!±

A temporary sacrifice in order to maintain the initiative. The move is based, as we shall see, on a hidden tactical point.

20 ... ♘xb5
21 ♗xe5 ♗e7?!

With time-pressure approaching, Black fails to put up the best resistance: 21 ... ♘e7? is easily dismissed in view of 22 ♘xb5 ♕xb5 23 ♕f3 ♖c8 24 ♕b7 ♕c6 25 ♗d6+-, however the true point of 20 ♖fe1! would be revealed only after **21 ... ♘xc3!** **22 ♗b8+!!** (22 ♗xc3+ ♘e7 is not so clear) **22 ... ♗e7 23 ♖d6!** and now:

a) **23 ... ♘f4** 24 ♖xe7+ ♔xe7 25 ♕h4+ f6 26 ♖xc6 ♘ce2+ 27 ♔f1 ♖axb8 28 ♖c7++-;

b) **23 ... ♕xd6!** 24 ♗xd6 ♘d5 25 ♗xe7! ♘dxe7 26 f4!±.

22 ♘xb5 0-0

On **22 ... ♕xb5**, 23 ♗xg7 ♖g8 24 ♕xh7 should win without much trouble.

23 ♘d4 ♕c5
24 b4! ♕c4

Taking the pawn would lose at least an exchange after 25 ♘c6. The game continuation allows White a brilliant finish.

25 ♘f5 ♗xb4 (95)

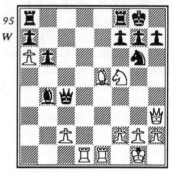

95
W

26 ♕h6! 1-0

It is mate next move.

Game 14
Kotronias - Khalifman
Moscow 1987

1 e4 c6 2 d4 d5 3 e5 ♗f5 4 ♘c3 ♕b6 5 ♗d3 ♗xd3 6 ♕xd3 e6 7 ♘ge2

7 ... ♘e7!

Black should opt for a flexible deployment of his pieces, before embarking on central operations. The alternative 7 ... ♕a6?! is of independent significance only after **8 ♕h3 b5** (8 ... ♘e7 is a direct transposition to the Main Game), but this is not particularly recommended. After **9 ♘f4**, both **9 ... c5** 10 dxc5 ♗xc5 11 0-0 12 ♘d3 ♗f8 13 ♘e2 ♘c6 14 ♘ef4, Bastriakov-Averbakh, USSR 1952, and **9 ...**

b4 10 ♘ce2 c5 11 dxc5 ♗xc5 12 ♘d3 ♕c4? 13 b3! ♕b5 14 0-0 ♗e7 15 a3, Kotronias-Skembris, Kavala Z 1985, leave Black struggling for survival.

On the other hand, a typical blunder after 8 ♕h3 would be **8 ... c5?** 9 ♘xd5! ♕a5+ 10 ♕c3 ♕xc3 11 ♘dxc3 ♘c6 12 ♗e3 cxd4 13 ♘xd4 ♘xd4 14 ♗xd4 ♗e7 15 ♘b5 ♘d5 16 c4+- Kotronias-Halldorson, Reykjavik 1988; if Black takes the offered knight by **9 ... exd5** there follows 10 ♕c8+ ♔e7 11 ♕xc5+ ♔e8 12 ♕c8+ ♔e7 13 b3! and White is winning.

    8   0-0   ♕a6?! *(96)*

This idea is not good, although it stems from Capablanca. Correct is **8 ... ♘d7 9 a4 a6** as in Kotronias-Tukmakov or **9 ... a5** 10 b3 h5 11 ♗g5 ♘f5 as in Kotronias-Orr (see the next Main Game). The queen is displaced on a6 and Black will soon have to admit his mistake by moving her again.

    9   ♕h3   ♘d7
    10   a4!

This position and similar ones have been discussed in Chapter 1 (mainly diagram 16). White's last move restricts the mobility of the black queen and serves positional purposes as well.

    10   ...   ♕b6!?

A novelty at the time, this move is better than 10 ... ♖c8 11 ♗e3 c5?! 12 ♘b5!± Mokry-Pedersen, Groningen 1977/8. Nevertheless, the text is an admission that the manoeuvre ... ♕b6-a6 was unsuccessful.

    11   b3?!

Vacillating. Correct is **11 a5!** ♕d8 12 ♘f4±. This position has been extensively analysed in Chapter 1 (diagram 30).

    11   ...   ♘f5
    12   a5   ♕d8
    13   ♘d1

The basic idea of this manoeuvre is 14 ♘e3 and the central break c2-c4, opening up the position.

    13   ...   c5
    14   c4

Black is OK in the complications which follow. However, the game features the proper antidote to an early ... c6-c5 and was a useful predecessor to Kotronias-Tukmakov (Game 15). This break is a typical reaction by White in such positions and is greatly aided by the position of the white queen on h3.

    14   ...   cxd4

After 14 ... dxc4 15 d5 White's

position is better than in the game, since the d1-knight is not obstructed by the enemy central pawn.

15	cxd5	♘xe5
16	dxe6	fxe6
17	♘f4	♕f6
18	♖e1	g6

During the game 18 ... ♗d6 looked better to me, since after 19 ♘h5?! ♕h4! 20 ♘xg7+ ♔d7 Black has a somewhat superior ending. However, there is the interesting alternative 19 ♖a2!? 0-0 20 ♖ae2, sacrificing a pawn for positional pressure.

19	♘d3

In this position the pawn sacrifice 19 ♖a2!? is also worth trying.

19	...	♗d6
20	♘xe5	♗xe5	(97)

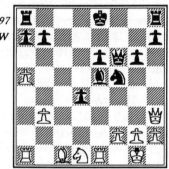

21	f4

Freeing the d1-knight for aggressive action, after which White stands a little better.

21	...	♗d6
22	♘f2	♗b4
23	♖e5	0-0
24	♗b2	

It is impossible to play 24

♘g4? ♕h4 and now 25 ♖xf5 is unplayable due to the back rank mate on e1.

24	...	♕f7
25	♘e4	♗e7
26	♖e1	♖ad8
27	♕d3	♖d5

Black chooses to return the pawn in order to activate his pieces.

28	♖xd5	exd5
29	♘g3	♘g7!

This is the only move, as 29 ... ♘xg3? 30 hxg3 ♗f6 31 ♗xd4 ♗xd4+ 32 ♕xd4 a6 33 ♖e5 ♖d8 34 g4 unnecessarily allows White to launch an attack.

30	♕xd4	♗f6
31	♕xf6	♕xf6
32	♗xf6	♖xf6
33	♘e2	♖e6
34	♔f2	♖e4
35	♖d1	♘e6
36	g3	

Naturally not 36 ♖xd5 ♖xe2+ and Black wins a piece.

36	...	♖b4
37	♖xd5	♖xb3
38	♖d7	♘c5
39	♖c7	♖b5
40	♖c8+	

The last trap, since now 40 ... ♔g7 41 ♘d4 ♖xa5 42 ♖xc5 wins a piece for White.

40	...	♔f7
41	♖c7+	½-½

Game 15
Kotronias – Tukmakov
Kavala 1991

1 e4 c6 2 d4 d5 3 e5 ♗f5 4

♘c3 ♕b6 5 ♗d3 ♗xd3 6
♕xd3 e6 7 ♘ge2 ♘e7 8 0-0

    8   ...   ♘d7
    9   a4   a6

The game Kotronias - Orr,
Dubai OL 1986, saw the double-
edged 9 ... a5!?, rendering the
advance ... c6-c5 dubious (because of the weakness of b5)
for the sake of maintaining the
pressure on d4. The game
continued 10 b3 h5 (preparing
... ♘e7-f5, as the immediate 10
... ♘f5 is met by 11 g4 ♘e7 12
♘g3 with the idea ♗c1-a3) 11
♗g5! (White perceives that his
adversary will have to spare a
tempo to exchange this bishop
himself by ... ♗f8-e7, so he
does not fall for 11 ♗a3 ♘f5
with a fine game for Black) 11
... ♘f5 12 ♖ad1 (98)

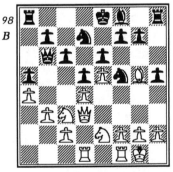

12 ... f6? (tension during an
Olympiad is far beyond the
ordinary, especially in last
round contests; here it caused
Black to lose his sense of
danger and commit a serious
error at the very beginning of
the game, while after the correct 12 ... ♗e7 13 ♗xe7 ♔xe7! the

fight would have just started)
13 exf6 gxf6 14 ♘f4!! (seizing
the opportunity to prevent
Black from castling; the Irish
master probably expected 14
♗c1 ♗d6 with an unclear position, but now White is just
winning) 14 ... fxg5 (14 ...
♕xd4 15 ♕h3 loses as well) 15
♘xe6 ♘e7 16 ♖fe1 (also possible is 16 ♕g3, but White prefers to apply direct pressure on
the hapless black monarch) 16
... ♖h6 17 ♕e2! (a multi-
purpose move, which prevents
17 ... ♖xe6 because of the continuation 18 ♕xh5+ ♔d8 19 ♖xe6
and at the same time prepares
to triple the major pieces along
the open e-file; the game is
practically over now) 17 ...
♕b4 18 ♖d3 ♕d6 (desperation,
but 18 ... ♖xe6 would have only
postponed the end) 19 ♖e3
♘f6 20 ♘xf8 ♔xf8 21 ♖xe7
♘e4 22 ♖e5 ♘f6 23 ♖xg5
♖e8 24 ♖e5 1-0.

    10   ♕h3   ♘f5
    11   a5   ♕d8
    12   ♘d1!   c5

Facing the positional threat
♘d1-e3 which will force the
exchange of Black's strong
knight on f5, the Ukrainian
Grandmaster hurries to show
some activity in the centre.
Taking into account Black's
lack of development, this approach is rather committal, but
not so much as 12 ... ♕h4 13
♕d3 c5 (Bjarke Kristensen
suggests 13 ... h5 followed by ...

g6 - Ed.) 14 c3 planning ♘f4±, Kotronias–K. Berg, Gausdal Troll Masters 1993.

13 c4!

White reacts in typical and at the same time effective fashion.

13 ... dxc4
14 d5 ♕h4

Unfortunately for Black, the threat to exchange queens is not enough to nullify White's initiative. With a series of unexpected queen manoeuvres, White manages not only to preserve, but actually to increase, the pressure.

15 dxe6 fxe6 *(99)*

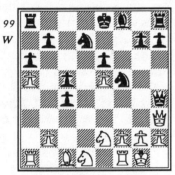

16 ♕c3! ♘d4
17 ♘xd4 ♕xd4
18 ♕h3 ♕xe5
19 ♘e3

The exchanges that have taken place favour White, since it is much easier for him to bring new forces into the battle. Besides, it is quite clear that Black will have problems both during the middlegame and in any ending with equal material, since the white knight on c4 is likely to dominate the proceedings.

19 ... ♗e7
20 ♘xc4 ♕e4?!

The continuation **20 ... ♕f5?** 21 ♕xf5 exf5 22 ♖e1+ ♔f7 23 ♗f4 threatening 24 ♖ad1 was highly undesirable, but Black's best was **20 ... ♕d5!** 21 b3! 0-0 (21 ... ♗f6?! 22 ♗b2 ♗xb2 23 ♘xb2±) 22 ♗b2 ♕f5 23 ♕g3 with an unclear position which, however, I consider more pleasant for White.

21 ♖a4 ♕c6
22 ♖e1 *(100)*

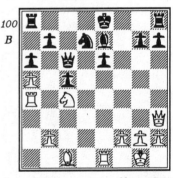

22 ... ♕xa4??

Black should seek salvation in an inferior endgame by **22 ... 0-0** 23 ♕xe6+ ♕xe6 24 ♖xe6±, but instead suffers an illusion with disastrous consequences. We have already had the chance to observe plenty of occasions where the defender tires of warding off alternating threats in different parts of the board.

23 ♕xe6 ♔d8

My opponent had overlooked that 23 ... 0-0-0 is dealt a death blow by 24 ♘b6+.

24 ♕xe7+ ♚c8
25 ♗f4 1-0

25 ...♕xc4 is met by 26 ♕e8+ with mate next move.

Conclusion

5 ♘d3!? is an interesting way to counter 4 ... ♛b6. Personal experience indicates that Black will have problems developing his pieces and achieving the liberating thrust ... c6-c5. Also, the games Kotronias–King and Kotronias–Tukmakov demonstrate that Black should avoid an early fight for the centre when White's lead in development could make itself felt. However, White players should be alert, as a slight mishandling can change the picture surprisingly quickly.

4 The 4 ... h5 Variation

Game 16
Nunn – Dlugy
London 1986

1 e4 c6 2 d4 d5 3 e5 ♗f5 4 ♘c3

4 ... h5?! *(101)*

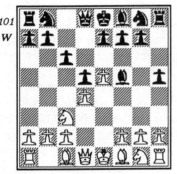

After White scored some beautiful wins employing the line 4 ♘c3 e6 5 g4 ♗g6 6 ♘ge2, Black players started searching for something new and less complicated. Given the benefit of hindsight, 4 ... h5?! is the most committal choice of all: White's kingside expansion is prevented, but at the cost of weakening the g5 square; Black also has to solve the problem of bringing his king into safety.

5 ♗d3!

White takes a first step towards shaking Black's control of f5. As a matter of principle, this is the only way to expose the weak side of 4 ... h5.

5	...	♗xd3
6	♕xd3	e6
7	♘f3	♘h6

Probably the best. For 7 ... ♕b6 see Game 17, Short–Seirawan.

8 0–0 ♘f5?!

This is a bit premature, inviting White's next move. Correct in my opinion is Nunn's **8 ... ♘d7** with the following possible continuations:

a) **9 ♖d1 c5** (9 ... ♘f5 10 ♘e2 c5 11 c4±) **10 ♗g5 c4** (10 ... ♕a5!? 11 dxc5 ♕xc5 {11 ... ♘xc5 12 ♕b5} 12 ♘e4 ♕c7 13 ♘d6+ ♗xd6 14 exd6 ♕c6 requires analysis) **11 ♗xd8 cxd3 12 ♗g5 dxc2 13 ♖dc1±**;

b) **9 ♘e2 c5 10 c4 dxc4 11 ♕xc4 ♘b6 12 ♕b5+ ♕d7 13 ♕xd7+ ♘xd7** (13 ... ♔xd7!?) **14 ♗xh6! ♖xh6 15 ♖ac1±**.

In both these lines the queens come off the board, but White keeps a slight advantage due to his better development.

9 ♘e2!

Continuing in the spirit of

his fifth move, White is ready to swap every piece that lands on f5, thus slowly denuding Black's kingside of its defenders.

9 ... ♘d7

In the game Glek-Vyzhmanavin, Lvov 1985, Black played **9 ... ♗e7** but after 10 b3 ♘d7 11 c4 ♘f8 12 ♗d2 ♘g6 13 c5 it became clear that he was lacking a constructive plan. This is an important example, showing that White can generate play on all parts of the board if the second player resorts to passive manoeuvres.

10 ♘g3

Also interesting is **10 ♖d1!?** with the idea b2-b3, c2-c4 but the text is more direct. Black now has to make a difficult choice.

10 ... ♘h4?! (102)

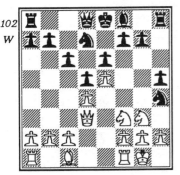

Opening up the f-file by **10 ... ♘xg3? 11 fxg3!** would be suicidal. However, better is Nunn's suggestion **10 ... g6!?** 11 ♘xf5 gxf5 12 ♗g5 ♗e7 13 h4 with a slight plus for White due to the weakness of the

h-pawn. The text neglects Black's development without good reason.

11 ♘xh4 ♕xh4
12 ♗e3 ♕d8
13 ♖fd1 ♖c8?

Better is 13 ... ♗e7, but White will continue similarly to Glek-Vyzhmanavin, gaining a big space advantage.

14 b3 c5?!

This move is consistent but wrong. Against a lesser opponent Dlugy might have got away with his plan, but objectively he should have reconciled himself to passive defence, starting with 14 ... ♗e7. As it is, Nunn is able to exploit Black's inaccuracies in a simple and powerful manner.

15 c4!± cxd4 (103)

Black is left with a choice of evils. Nunn analyses: **15 ... h4** (15 ... ♘b6 16 dxc5 ♗xc5 17 ♗xc5 ♖xc5 18 ♘e4±) **16 ♘e2** (16 cxd5!? hxg3 17 dxe6 ♘xe5 18 dxe5 ♕xd3 19 exf7 ♔xf7 20 ♖xd3±) and now:

a) **16 ... ♘b6** 17 ♖ac1 dxc4 18 bxc4 cxd4 19 ♘xd4 ♗c5 20 ♕e4 ♕e7 21 ♕g4±;

b) **16 ... dxc4** 17 ♕xc4 cxd4 18 ♕xd4 ♗c5 19 ♕e4 ♗xe3 20 ♕xe3±.

16 cxd5! ♘xe5

After 16 ... dxe3 17 dxe6 Black has no defence to the numerous threats. It is in this variation that the weaknesses created by ... h7-h5 become particularly glaring.

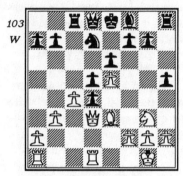

103
W

17 ♕xd4   ♕xd5?

Losing at once, but **17 ...
♘g4** 18 ♕xa7 could only prolong resistance.

18   ♕a4+   1-0

Black resigned, since 18 ...
♕c6 19 ♖ac1! leaves White a
clear rook ahead.

Game 17
Short – Seirawan
Rotterdam 1989

**1 e4 c6 2 d4 d5 3 e5 ♗f5 4
♘c3 h5?! 5 ♗d3! ♗xd3 6
♕xd3 e6 7 ♘f3**

7   ...   ♕b6

Seirawan tries a different
approach in comparison to the
previous game; the king will
hide on the queenside, while in
the centre Black prepares to
strike with ... f7-f6. However,
in my opinion, his plan lacks
chances of success for two
reasons: firstly, the black king
castles opposite a mobile pawn
mass, ready to advance at the
earliest opportunity; secondly,
his counterplay in the centre
will merely create a backward

e-pawn which is very difficult
to advance without creating
further weaknesses. ♕a6

8   0-0   ♕a6

Seirawan suggests **8 ...
♘e7!?** and **8 ... ♘d7** which
both bear a close resemblance
to lines in Chapter 3. The only
differences are the placement
of White's king's knight and
the advancement of Black's
h-pawn, but I do not think
these facts can drastically alter
the evaluation of the position.

9   ♕d1

White's loss of time is only
apparent, since the black queen
is far away from the centre and
will need to move again in
order to rejoin the action.

9   ...   ♘e7

10   ♘e2

A typical motif that has been
encountered in several cases in
this book. White is ready to
swap knights with ♘e2-g3,
after Black's knight arrives on
f5.

10   ...   ♘d7

11   c3   ♘f5

12   ♗g5   ♗e7

13   ♘g3!   ♘xg3

On **13 ... g6** the automatic
reaction would be 14 ♘xf5 gxf5
15 h4, permanently fixing the
weakness on h5.

14   fxg3   f6

White's pressure along the
f-file forces this pawn action
which, although undoubtedly
planned beforehand, cannot be
sufficiently supported by pieces

and thus creates more weaknesses than counterplay.

15	exf6	gxf6
16	♗f4	0-0-0
17	♖e1	♘f8 (104)

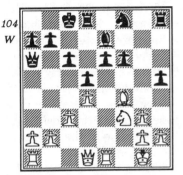

The black knight occupies a passive position on the back rank, while the rest of his pieces are also not conveniently placed. Black's inactive stance encourages White to expand immediately on the queenside.

18 b4!

Ruling out ... c6–c5, and preparing to open lines against the black king. Seirawan, realizing how perilous the situation is becoming, decides to bring his queen back into play.

18	...	♕b6!
19	a4	♗d6
20	♕d2	♕c7
21	b5	♖h7!

The only move. Not only does it defend the second rank, it also prepares ... ♖h7-e7 giving his e-pawn ample protection. Now Short has to work hard to get something tangible.

22 ♗xd6! ♕xd6

On 22 ... ♖xd6 23 ♕f4±

(Cabrilo). But now the black queen is also lured away from controlling e5.

| 23 | bxc6 | ♕xc6 |
| 24 | ♕f4 | |

White again occupies the fatal diagonal, this time with his queen and, very significantly, with tempo.

24 ... ♘d7 (105)

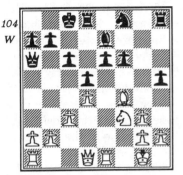

25 ♔h1!

White would like to play 25 ♖ac1 ♖e7 26 c4 dxc4 27 d5 but this fails because of 27 ... ♕c5+!. Having realized this, Short sets his opponent a cunning trap ...

25 ... ♖e7!

... which is spotted immediately. Black prepares to block the dangerous h2-b8 diagonal if, and when, appropriate.

26	a5	e5
27	♕f5	♔b8
28	♕xh5	♕xc3
29	♕f5	♖de8
30	♖ec1	

White holds a slight advantage due to his safer king, better endgame prospects and strongly-placed queen on f5, but Black is not totally devoid of resources. However, his next move (instead of the solid **30 ... ♛b4!** to be followed by 31 ... ♛d6 as recommended by Cabrilo) unwisely removes the queen from the defence, allowing Short to start a fierce attack.

	30 ...	♛e3?
	31 ♛c2!	

Ensuring the penetration of White's pieces. Black resists well, but Short leaves him no chances.

	31 ...	♚a8
	32 a6	♞b6
	33 axb7+	♜xb7
	34 dxe5	fxe5
	35 ♜e1	♛h6
	36 ♞xe5	♜be7 *(106)*

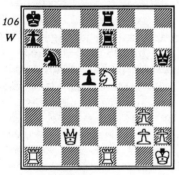

37 ♜eb1!

A Greek gift. If Black takes the proffered knight by 37 ...

♜xe5, then 38 ♛c7 decides the outcome immediately.

	37 ...	♜b7
	38 ♞c6	♛e3
	39 ♞xa7!	

The concluding blow, after which Black has no hope left (39 ... ♚xa7 40 ♜xa7+ ♚xa7 41 ♛c7+♚a8 is followed not by 42 ♛xb6 ♛e1+, but 42 ♜a1+ with immediate mate).

	39 ...	♚b8
	40 ♞c6+	♚c8
	41 ♞e7++	♚d8
	42 ♞xd5!	1-0

Black decided that the white knight had danced enough.

Conclusion

The line with 4 ... h5?! is extremely dangerous for Black since important positional concessions are made without any tangible gain. As far as practice has shown, White is able to capitalize on his development and space advantage, a well-timed c2-c4 usually being the main idea. Apparently, there is no satisfactory path for Black to equalize, but 7 ... ♞h6 8 0-0 ♞d7 should be tested in serious competition before a final verdict is reached.

5 The 4 ... ♕d7/c8 Variation

Game 18
Van der Wiel – Hort
Wijk aan Zee 1986

1 e4 c6 2 d4 d5 3 e5 ♗f5 4 ♘c3

4 ... ♕d7 *(107)*

This move has been adopted on a regular basis by GM Vlastimil Hort. Together with 4 ... ♕c8, it serves to prevent g2–g4 without weakening Black's pawn skeleton. Although this plan looks artificial, White has been unable so far to prove a considerable advantage.

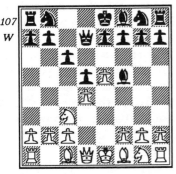

5 ♗e3

An alternative that has been tried successfully here is **5 ♘f3**. The game Schmittdiel-Serrer, German Ch 1991, continued 5 ... e6 6 ♘h4 ♗g6 7 ♗e3 ♕c7 8 f4 a6?! *(108)*

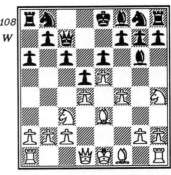

9 f5! ♗xf5 10 ♘xf5 exf5 11 ♗d3 g6 12 g4± fxg4 13 ♕xg4 ♕d7 14 ♕f3 ♘h6 15 0-0-0 ♗xe3+ 16 ♕xe3 ♕e7 17 h4 ♘d7 18 h5 gxh5 19 ♖xh5 0-0-0 20 ♗f5 b5 21 ♕g3 f6 22 ♖e1 ♕f7 23 ♘g4 fxe5 24 dxe5 ♕e7 25 ♘e2 ♔b7 26 ♘f4 ♘f8 27 ♘d3 ♘h6?? 28 ♖xh6 ♕g5+ 29 ♕f4 1-0. However, Black should not have allowed 9 f5 (thus **8 ... ♘e7**).

5 ... h6

Nunn-Hort, Lugano 1987, continued 5 ... h5 6 ♘f3 ♘h6 7 h3 e6 8 ♗e2 ♗e7 9 ♕d2 b5 10 ♗g5 a5 11 ♖c1 ♕d8 12 a4 b4 13 ♘d1 ♘a6 14 0-0 ♗g6 15 ♕f4 ♘f5 16 ♗xe7 ♘xe7 17 ♘e3 ♕b6 18 ♖fd1 0-0-0 19 ♘h4 ♖d7 20 ♘xg6 ♘xg6 21 ♕g5 with White enjoying a slight advantage, according to Seirawan.

    6   h3!?

    6 ♗d3!? ♗xd3 7 ♕xd3 e6 8 ♘ge2 ♘e7 (8 ... c5 9 dxc5 ♘a6 10 c6! ♕xc6 11 ♘d4±) **9 0-0 ♘f5 10 ♘g3±** is a quieter approach.

    6   ...   e6
    7   g4   ♗h7
    8   f4   ♗b4

Black declares his intentions: he is planning an harmonious development of his knights to e7 and d7, followed by ... 0-0-0. The only disadvantage of this scheme is that sooner or later Black has to part with his valuable dark-squared bishop.

    9   ♘ge2   ♘e7

The theoretical duel between Nunn and Hort had started earlier (Bundesliga 1983/4), with **9 ... ♘a6 10 ♘g3 ♘c7 11 a3 ♗e7**, also assessed as slightly better for White by Seirawan.

    10   a3   ♗xc3+
    11   ♘xc3   ♕c7
    12   ♗d3

While this surrenders the advantage of the two bishops, it is difficult to find an alternative plan for White. The type of pawn structure suggests that the only way to cause Black serious worries is by enforcing the advance f4-f5.

    12   ...   ♘d7
    13   ♗xh7   ♖xh7
    14   ♕d3   g6
    15   ♗f2   ♖g7! *(109)*

This clever move creates obstacles in White's path but I think that with accurate play

some advantage can still be hoped for.

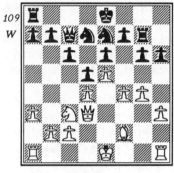

109
W

    16   0-0-0

As this does not lead to anything special, I propose here the continuation **16 ♘e2!?** (the knight protects g3 in preparation for ♗f2-h4) **16 ... 0-0-0** (on 16 ... c5 White replies 17 dxc5 ♘xc5 18 ♕c3 and now either 18 ... ♘a6 19 ♕xc7 ♘xc7 20 ♘d4 ♔d7 21 a4! with a slight advantage in the ending or 18 ... ♖c8 19 0-0-0 b6 20 ♘g3 with White enjoying some initiative) **17 ♗h4 g5 18 f5! gxh4** (18 ... exf5 19 gxf5 gxh4 20 f6 is good for White, but now the point of 16 ♘e2!? is revealed since the move ... ♖g7-g3 is no longer possible) **19 f6 ♖g6** (19 ... ♖7g8 20 fxe7 ♖de8 21 ♕h7!) **20 fxe7 ♖e8 21 ♖f1!** with a slight advantage for White.

    16   ...   0-0-0

The position is equal.

    17   ♖df1!?

Wrong is 17 ♗h4 g5 18 f5? gxh4 19 f6 ♘xf6 20 exf6 ♕f4+, according to the Dutch IM Pieterse.

17 ... a6
18 ♗h4 ♖e8

Black has satisfactory play by simple means, therefore Hort refrains from ideas like **18 ... g5!?** 19 f5 ♖gg8 (planning ... c6-c5) with unclear play (Seirawan).

19	f5	gxf5
20	♗xe7	♖xe7
21	gxf5	♖e8
22	♖hg1	♖xg1
23	♖xg1	c5
24	fxe6	fxe6
25	♕g6	♔d8
26	♕f7	cxd4
27	♖g8	♖xg8
28	♕xg8+	♔e7
29	♕h7+	♔d8

½-½

Game 19
Kotronias – Skembris
Athens (4th Match Game)
1987

1 e4 c6 2 d4 d5 3 e5 ♗f5 4 ♘c3

4 ... ♕c8

In Timman-Speelman, Reykjavik 1991, Black experimented with **4 ... a6!?**, achieving an excellent position after **5 ♗e3 ♕c7 6 ♘ge2 e6 7 ♘g3 ♗e7 8 ♘xf5?** ♗xf5 9 ♗d3 ♗xe3 10 fxe3 c5; although this is given as equal by Seirawan, I believe that White has already ruined his chances, a fact convincingly confirmed by the game continuation: 11 ♕g4 ♘c6 12 0-0-0 0-0-0 13 ♖hf1 h5 14 ♕h4?!

♗e7∓ 15 ♕f4? cxd4 16 exd4 f6 17 ♖fe1 ♔b8 18 ♗f1 fxe5 19 dxe5 ♘f6-+ 20 g3 ♗xe5 21 ♕g5 h4 22 ♕g4 hxg3 23 hxg3 ♗xc3 24 bxc3 e5 25 ♕g5 ♕a5 26 ♔b2 ♖h2 27 ♖xe5 ♘xe5 28 ♕xe5+ ♕c7 29 ♕xc7+ ♔xc7 30 ♖d4 g5 31 ♖g4 ♖g8 32 ♖d4 ♖f2 33 ♗h3 ♖g6 and 0-1. Nevertheless, **6 ♗d3** ♗xd3 7 cxd3!? e6 8 ♖c1 is slightly better for White, according to Speelman.

5	♗e3	g6
6	♕d2	♘d7
7	♘ge2	h5
8	♘g3	♗e6?!

Also bad is **8 ... ♘b6?** 9 ♘xf5 ♕xf5 10 b4 (even better than 10 a4!?) a5 11 ♖a3 e6 12 ♖b3 ♗b4 13 ♗d3 ♘c4 14 ♖c1 ♕g4 15 0-0 and the white rook's unusual position on b3 is more of a strength than a weakness, if only because of the unsatisfactory cooperation of Black's forces) 10 ... ♕d7 11 a4 e6 (or 11 ... a5 12 bxa5 ♖xa5 13 e6 fxe6 14 ♗d3 with a strong attack for White) 12 a5 ♘c8 13 ♘e2 and the plan ♘e2-f4-d3-c5 guarantees White an advantage. Comparatively best seems **8 ... e6** 9 ♘xf5 gxf5 10 ♘e2 c5 11 c3 h4 12 ♘f4 with White enjoying only a small superiority.

9	♗d3	♘b6
10	a4	h4
11	♘ge2	♗f5?!

Better is **11 ... a5** 12 ♖a3 ♖a7 followed by ... ♘b6-a8-c7.

12	a5	♘c4

Not **12 ... ♗xd3?** 13 cxd3 ♘d7

14 e6 and White is already winning.

13	♗xc4	dxc4
14	0-0	♗h6
15	♖a4	♗e6
16	♗xh6?!	

Superior is 16 ♖d1!.

16	...	♘xh6
17	♘f4	♘f5
18	♖d1± *(110)*	

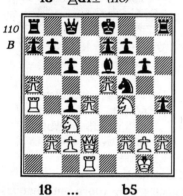

18 ... b5

This is the only move to continue fighting, at least in a practical sense; for example, after 18 ... 0-0? 19 ♘xe6 ♕xe6 20 ♕e2 the game is beyond salvation.

19	axb6	axb6
20	♖xa8	♕xa8
21	♘xe6	fxe6
22	♕e2	

White has a big advantage, but it is still not so easy to bring it home.

22	...	b5
23	♘e4	0-0
24	♕g4	♔g7
25	♘c5	♔f7
26	♕f3	♕d8!

Skembris manages to set a few traps, e.g. here 27 ♕xc6?

♕d5 28 ♕xd5 exd5 29 c3 ♖a8 and Black has achieved some counterplay.

27	c3	♕d5 *(111)*

[Chessboard diagram 111, White to move]

28 ♕h3!

With the idea 28 ... ♖a8? 29 g4! hxg3 30 ♕h7+ ♘g7 31 fxg3+-. Black does not have adequate improvements in this variation, for example 29 ... ♘h6 30 ♕e3 or 29 ... ♘g7 30 ♕xh4 planning ♖e1 and ♘e4. Normally the end should be near now, as White conquers the a-file for his rook.

28	...	♔g7
29	♖a1	b4
30	♕g4	bxc3
31	bxc3	♖b8
32	h3	♖b5
33	♕f4	♔f7
34	♖a7	♕d8
35	♘e4?	

Jeopardizing the win in time trouble. Immediately decisive was 35 ♕g5 (threatening 36 ♕f6+) 35 ... ♕h8 36 ♘xe6 etc.

35	...	♖b1+
36	♔h2	♕b8
37	♘g5+??	

Continuing in the same

direction; 37 ♘d6+! was enough to achieve the desired objective, e.g. 37 ... ♔g8 38 ♖xe7! ♘xe7 39 ♕f7+ ♔h8 40 ♕f6+ ♔g8 41 ♕xe6+ ♔h8 42 ♕xe7 or 37 ... ♔f8 38 ♘xf5 ♕xa7 39 ♘d6+ with an easily winning position.

37	...	♔e8
38	♖a6	♔d7
39	♘e4	♖e1
40	♘d2	♕b7
41	♖a2±	♔c7?

White has still kept a considerable advantage, but it was possible to continue fighting through **41 ... ♔e8** 42 ♘f3! ♖h1+ (the only serious try) 43 ♔xh1 ♕b1+ 44 ♔h2 ♕xa2 45 ♘g5! ♔d7 46 ♕f3! ♕a5 (the variations 46 ... ♕c2 47 ♘h7 and 46 ... ♕a8 47 ♘e4 ♔e8 48 ♕g4 ♔f7 49 ♘g5+ lose simply) 47 ♘e4 ♕d5 48 ♕g4 and despite White's obvious superiority the game is not over yet.

42	♕g4	g5
43	♕xg5	♖e2 *(112)*
44	♕g8!	♖xf2
45	♕xe6	♕b8

Or 45 ... ♘e3 46 ♕xe7+ ♔c8

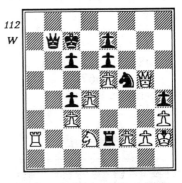

112
W

47 ♕xb7+ ♔xb7 48 ♖b2+ ♔c7 49 ♘xc4 etc.

46 d5

The rest is pretty clear.

46	...	cxd5
47	♕xd5	♕b6
48	♘xc4	1-0

Conclusion

Black's 4th move alternatives are not to be taken lightly; nothing has been refuted and nothing has been explored well. However, Speelman's 4 ... a6!? looks more useful than 4 ... ♕d7/c8, and only further encounters can show what is the best plan for White.

6　The 3 ... c5 Variation

Game 20
Tal – Botvinnik
Moscow (8th Match Game)
1961

1 e4 c6 2 d4 d5 3 e5

3　...　c5 *(113)*

This move became fashionable in the early 1960s when Botvinnik employed it in several World Championship games against Tal. Nowadays it is a rare bird in tournament practice since it has been long established that White can get an advantage in a variety of ways.

4　dxc5　e6

For 4 ... ♘c6 see Game 21.

5　♕g4!?

Some old analysis by Boleslavsky runs **5 ♗e3!** ♘e7 6 c3 ♘f5 7 ♗d4 and now after either

7 ... ♕c7 8 ♗d3 ♘xc5 9 ♗xc5 ♕xc5 10 ♗xf5 exf5 11 ♘f3 ♘c6 12.0-0 0-0 13 ♘bd2 or **7 ... ♘xd4** 8 cxd4 b6 9 b4 a5 10 ♗b5 ♗d7 11 ♕a4 White's superiority is evident.

In the 4th game of the same match Tal explored **5 ♘c3**, but the result was less successful: 5 ... ♘c6 6 ♗f4 ♘ge7 7 ♘f3 ♘g6 8 ♗e3 ♘gxe5 9 ♘xe5 ♘xe5 10 ♕h5 ♘c6 11 0-0-0 ♗e7 12 f4 g6 13 ♕h6 ♗f8 14 ♕g5 ♕xg5 15 fxg5 h6 16 ♘a4 ♗d7 17 ♗f4 a6 18 ♘b6 ♖d8 19 ♗c7 hxg5 20 c4 d4 21 b4 ♗g7 22 ♗xd8 ♔xd8 23 b5 ♘b8 24 ♗e2 *(114)*

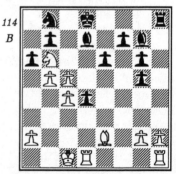

24 ... f5 25 ♗f3 axb5 26 cxb5 ♗xb5 27 ♗xb7 ♔c7 28 a4 ♗xa4 29 ♘xa4 ♔xb7 30 ♔d2 ♘d7 31 ♖b1+ ♔c6 32 ♖hc1 ♗e5 33 ♔d3 ♖a8 34 ♖b6+ ♘xb6 35 cxb6+

♗d7 36 ♘c5+ ♔e7 37 ♖e1 ♖a3+ 38 ♔c4 ♖c3+ 39 ♔b5 ♖e3 40 ♖a1 ♗xh2 41 ♖a7+ ♔e8 and ½–½. My conclusion is that 5 ♘c3 is rather inconsistent and worthless from the theoretical point of view.

| 5 | ... | ♘c6 |

5 ... h5!? is a likely improvement here, so Boleslavsky's analysis is more to be trusted. It is also possible to regain the pawn immediately with 5 ... ♘d7 6 ♗b5 ♕c7. The text is a dubious idea which underestimates White's tactical possibilities.

6	♘f3	♕c7
7	♗b5	♗d7
8	♗xc6!	

White's position contains many strongpoints to compensate for the bishop pair. Black's tempo loss in the opening allows Tal to carry out typically Nimzowitschian ideas in exemplary fashion.

| 8 | ... | ♕xc6 |
| 9 | ♗e3 | |

White not only has an extra pawn but is also ahead in development. Therefore Botvinnik decides to regain the material at the cost of deteriorating his pawn structure.

| 9 | ... | ♘h6 |
| 10 | ♗xh6! | |

The second bishop goes, but White has correctly judged that in the resulting position Black cannot effectively use his bishops because of his backward development. On the contrary, the white knights have excellent squares from which to operate.

| 10 | ... | gxh6 |

The advantage of the open g-file is offset by the insecurity of the black king and the weakened pawn structure. Practically, Black is facing insurmountable problems in such positions.

| 11 | ♘bd2 | ♕xc5 |
| 12 | c4! | |

Predicting ... 0-0-0, Tal is quick to open up the game. White's central control guarantees that Black's bishops will not be dangerous.

12	...	0-0-0
13	0-0	♔b8
14	♖fd1	♕b6
15	♕h4!	

Tal is piling on the pressure with quiet moves. The text keeps an eye on d8 and h6, while at the same time protecting his own potential weakness on f2. It should be noted that the light-squared bishop's future is also hampered since the valuable e7 square is also controlled.

| 15 | ... | a5 |

Trying to blockade the queenside, but the impression is that this rather invites White to attack. Preferable is 15 ... ♖e8 or 15 ... ♖g8 when Black can still fight.

| 16 | ♖ac1 | ♖g8 |

The game continuation

suggests that immediately **16 ... a4** was better.

17 ♘b3   a4

Black cannot play **17 ... dxc4 18 ♖xc4** when the pin on the d-file will win material for White. However, it was possible to open up the game for the bishops with **17 ... ♖c8 18 cxd5 ♖xc1 19 ♘xc1 exd5 20 ♖xd5 ♗c6** and Black keeps some practical hopes alive.

18 c5

This move creates the kind of semi-blocked position which reveals the power of knights over bishops; taking advantage of the strongpoint at d4, White can expand on the queenside at will.

18 ...   ♕c7
19 ♘bd4   ♖c8 *(115)*

20 b4   axb3
21 axb3   ♕d8

Botvinnik tries to take the sting out of White's attack by exchanging queens, but here White is so superbly placed that he can happily agree to this. Anyway, Black could hardly find anything better in view of his miserable king position and White's queenside pawn majority.

22 ♕xd8   ♖xd8
23 b4   ♖g4
24 b5   ♖c8
25 c6

White's forceful pawn advance, aided by his whole army, cannot be stopped by Black. The most important rôle is played by the knight on d4, a superb blockader.

26 ♖c2   ♗g7

The bishop's entrance to the game comes too late to change the outcome. White's forces on the queenside are already poised to deliver the knock-out blow and the a-file is about to have its say.

27 ♖a1   ♗xe5?

27 ... ♖xd4 was the only way to prolong resistance, but White still wins after **28 ♘xd4 ♗xe5 29 ♖ca2! ♗xd4 30 ♖a8+ ♔c7 31 ♖xc8+ ♔xc8 32 ♖a8+ ♔c7 33 cxb7** etc.

28 ♘xe5   ♖xd4
29 ♘d7+!   1-0

Not waiting for **29 ... ♗xd7** (even worse is **29 ... ♔c7 30 b6+ ♔d8 31 cxb7) 30 cxd7 ♖d8 31 ♖c8+! ♖xc8 32 ♖a8+!** when White sweeps away the whole black army at one stroke.

Game 21
Shabalov – K. Arkell
London 1991

1 e4 c6 2 d4 d5 3 e5

3   ...   c5

At this point, Black's lesser alternatives are, to say the least, dubious. For the sake of completeness we shall take a quick look at one of them:

a) **3 ... ♘a6?!** (what is the idea?), after which I recommend **4 ♘d2 ♕b6** (4 ... ♘c7 5 ♗d3±) 5 c3 (with the idea b2-b4) 5 ... c5 6 dxc5 ♘xc5 7 ♘b3 ♘xb3 8 axb3 and White is clearly better.

Against 3 ... ♘a6 Nunn has twice essayed the immediate **4 c3** with good results. The game Nunn-Nikolac, Bundesliga 1984, continued **4 ... ♗f5** 5 ♘e2 e6 6 ♘f4 ♘e7 7 ♘d2 ♘c7 8 g4 ♗g6 9 h4 f6 10 ♘xg6 hxg6 11 ♘f3 ♕d7 12 ♖g1 0-0-0 13 ♗d3 c5 14 ♗f4 cxd4 15 cxd4 ♘c6 16 ♗xg6 ♗b4+ 17 ♔f1 ♖df8 18 h5 *(116)*

18 ... fxe5 19 ♘xe5 ♘xe5 20 ♗xe5 ♗d6 21 ♕e2 ♗xe5 22 ♕xe5 ♕b5+ 23 ♔g2 ♕xb2 24 ♖gf1 ♕a3 25 f4 ♕e7 26 ♖ac1 ♖d8 27 f5 ♕d6 28 fxe6 ♕xe5 29 dxe5 ♔b8 30 e7 ♖dg8 31 ♗f7 ♖c8 32 g5 d4 33 ♖fd1 and 1-0, while Nunn-K.

Arkell, London 1990, saw **4 ...** ♘c7 5 ♘e2 (5 ♗d3 g6 6 ♘d2 {6 ♘f3!?} 6 ... h5 7 ♘f1 {7 ♘df3!?} 7 ... ♘h6 8 ♘a3 ♘g4 9 ♘f3 ♘xe3 10 fxe3 ♗f5= was van der Wiel-Kavalek, Wijk aan Zee 1982, but White could keep a slight advantage with 10 ♗xe3, according to Seirawan) 5 ... g6 6 ♘g3 ♘h6 7 ♘d2 ♗g4 8 f3 ♗d7 9 f4 ♘e6 10 ♘f3 ♗g7 11 h3 ♘hf5 12 ♘xf5 ♗xf5 13 g4 ♗e4 14 ♖g1 f5 15 ♘g5 e6 16 ♕b3 ♕d7 17 ♗e3 ♗e7 18 ♘xe4 fxe4 19 0-0-0 0-0-0 20 c4 ♔b8 21 c5 with a clear advantage for White, according to Speelman, although Black eventually managed to draw.

4   dxc5   ♘c6
5   ♗b5

This is Boleslavsky's suggestion, while inferior seems **5 ♘f3**, after which the game Kirov-K. Arkell, Leningrad 1989, progressed as follows: 5 ... ♗g4 6 ♗b5 ♕a5+ 7 ♘c3 e6 8 ♗e3 a6 9 ♗xc6+ bxc6 10 a3 ♗xf3 11 ♕xf3 ♗xc5 12 0-0 ♗xe3 13 ♕xe3 ♘e7 14 b4 ♕c7 15 ♘a4 a5 16 ♘c5 0-0 17 ♘b3 axb4 18 axb4 ♘f5 19 ♕c3 ♕b6 20 ♖xa8 ♖xa8 21 ♖a1 ♖xa1+ 22 ♕xa1 ♕xb4 23 ♕a8+ ♕f8 24 ♕xc6 h5 with a slight advantage for Black (eventually converted to a win after another 24 moves).

5   ...   ♕a5+
6   ♘c3   e6
7   ♗e3   ♘e7

The old analysis by Boleslavsky runs **7 ... ♗d7 8 ♘f3**

(also interesting is Pachman's 8 ♘xc6 ♗xc6 9 ♘f3 ♗xc5 10 ♗xc5 ♕xc5 11 ♕d4± - see Chapter 1, diagram 18) 8 ... ♘xe5 (8 ... ♘ge7 9 a3 ♘g6 10 ♗xc6 ♗xc6 11 ♗d4±) 9 ♘xe5 ♗xb5 10 ♕h5 g6 11 ♘xg6 ♘f6 12 ♕h4 ♘e4 13 ♘xf8 and White has a clear plus.

8 ♘f3 ♘f5 *(117)*

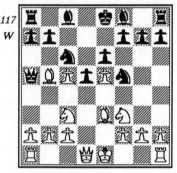

117 W

9 a3!±

As often happens in the Caro Advance, the specific requirements of the position demand that White spoil his pawn formation; in compensation, the dynamism of his position increases considerably. And just have a look at the c8-bishop, which Black's very first move planned to liberate!

9 ... ♘xe3
10 fxe3 ♕c7
11 e4

A most unusual break by White in this variation, all the more effective for this reason.

11 ... dxe4
12 ♘xe4 ♗xc5

Black has no option, but forcing tactics from a position with fewer developed pieces can only lead to a hopeless situation.

13 ♘xc5 ♕a5+
14 b4 ♕xb5
15 ♕d6 a5

Useless action, since opening up the a-file would only benefit White. Although he could hardly hope to save himself in the long run, Black's best was to initiate the plan he chooses next move by 15 ... ♘e7, e.g. 16 ♖d1 ♕b6 with just a few practical chances.

16 ♔f2 ♘e7
17 ♖hd1 ♘d5 *(118)*

Now 17 ... ♕b6 is impossible, but Black has deluded himself that he has built a fortress.

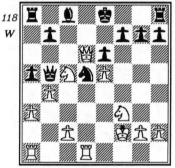

118 W

18 c4!

Such blows almost always exist in the Caro Advance when White has a lead in development.

18 ... ♕xc4
19 ♖ac1 ♕a2+
20 ♔g3

As if to demonstrate Black's inability to undertake anything even resembling counterplay.

20	...	axb4
21	♘a6	

The final conclusive blow, threatening above all 22 ♖xd5.

21	...	bxa6

22	♖c7	1-0

Black is not given any hope with 22 ♕c6+, while now the renewed threat 23 ♖xd5 spells the end.

Index of Complete Games

(Main Games in italics)

Index of Partial Games

Index of Variations